P9-CFX-466

Calum's Road

The publisher would like to dedicate
this book to Joyce McLelland (1921–2006),
an extraordinary person who was loved
by all who knew her

Calum's Road

Roger Hutchinson

BIRLINN

First published in 2006 by
Birlinn Limited
West Newington House
10 Newington Road
Edinburgh
EH9 1QS

10 9 8 7 6 5 4

www.birlinn.co.uk

ISBN10: 1 84158 447 9
ISBN13: 978 1 84158 447 8

British Library Cataloguing-in-Publication Data
A catalogue record for this book is available from the British Library

Designed and Typeset by Hewer Text UK Ltd, Edinburgh
Printed and bound by Creative Print and Design, Wales

Do mhuinntir Ratharsair, na bh'ann,
na th'ann 's na tha ri teachd

Contents

Preface

In February 1979 I had been working as a journalist on a Highland newspaper for fifteen months. There arrived in the editorial office notification of some council work that was apparently due to commence on a crofter's homemade track in the island of Raasay. It was, I was told, a good story.

I took the small car ferry from Sconser in Skye to Raasay. I then motored up a long and winding single-track road to Brochel Castle in the north of the island. I took the car up a short, steep hill past Brochel and saw ahead of me an apparently limitless expanse of peat bog, heather and granite. A grey road wound across this solitude and disappeared out of sight. It was a perfectly good stone-based road – wide and gently contoured – but it had no tarmacadam topping. As a result it consisted of two parallel wheel tracks and a large central ridge inside trim rocky verges. The wheel tracks were worn and rutted with use. The central ridge was pronounced and studded with sharp stones that seemed likely to remove any ordinarily slung exhaust pipe. I could not realistically contemplate driving any further, and so I parked and looked around.

I knew from the map that this was the road in question and that the relevant crofter lived almost two miles further along it. It was cold and beginning to rain. It would soon be dark. The last ferry back to Skye would leave in little over an hour. I looked around the silent emptiness, shivered and resigned myself to missing the road's maker.

Then there was some movement among the trees and shrubbery down the hillside to my right. A wiry man, five feet eight inches tall, walked easily up out of the vegetation, smiled at me shyly and offered his hand. He was, he said, Calum MacLeod.

He had a weather-worn telegraph pole balanced on his right shoulder. He had found it washed up on the shore – he pointed several hundred feet below us – and thought that it might be useful. I suppose we talked for fifteen or twenty minutes, but he did not rest the pole upon the ground, or show any indication of needing or wanting to put it down, until I asked to take his photograph. At that point he dropped it smartly and struck an experienced pose for the camera.

I now know that Calum was sixty-seven years old at that time, and I cannot say that he looked much younger. His face, beneath a battered tartan bonnet, carried the wear of a hard life spent out of doors. But I knew well enough that I, forty years younger than

Calum MacLeod, could not in my late twenties, nor at any time after, have carried that telegraph pole even ten yards up the slope below us. If I had managed to move it five paces I would then have seized any opportunity or none to drop it and take a very long rest. 'He was hardy, boy, was Calum', as a shared acquaintance would say. 'There was not an ounce of spare flesh on him.'

Calum told me about his road. He told me of the requests made in the 1920s to Inverness County Council by his parents and another ninety adults for a road. He told me – as he would tell so many others, in a tone that wavered between wry amusement and disgust – of how the council 'kept putting it off and putting it off, until one after another of the young families left because there seemed to be no prospect of a cart road, and eventually there was nobody left but myself and my wife'.

He told me of his eventual conclusion, in 1964 – that was the year which he cited to me in 1979 – that if he did not build a road between Brochel and Arnish then nobody else would.

Not many months after that encounter I walked the length of Calum's road for the first time. It was a glorious early summer's day, but the one and three quarter miles appeared to be unnaturally long. Its surface was as before – which is to say that only the wheel ruts and the rugged central ridge prevented a car from traversing it – and it made for relatively easy hiking. But the terrain gave, and still gives, this high-

way epic proportions. Rarely can more than a quarter of a mile of Calum's road be seen in any single stretch. Everywhere its next section disappears elusively from sight, around bends in the cliff-face, or down into glens, or off over hilltops. One and three quarter miles of a motorway (or, as Calum himself would say, of an autobahn) is as quickly traversed as it is seen. One and three quarter miles of the road between Brochel and Arnish is like an odyssey.

And later I walked it again. And later still I drove one motorcar after another along it. With every passage it seemed increasingly not only to represent some kind of heroic last stand but also to be a parable. Not a myth or fable, for it is firmly grounded in fact, but a simple morality tale.

The test of its allegorical power would be, of course, endurance. Like good roads, parables not only survive the passing of the years but grow stronger with them. And Calum's road has established itself effortlessly in the folklore first of the Highlands and Islands and then of Scotland, and steadily thereafter of the United Kingdom and the whole great wider world beyond Loch Arnish. A curious physical process seemed to be under way in which as the Gaelic Hebridean society which Calum MacLeod fought for, embodied and loved slipped into history so his immense, defiant gesture became increasingly significant. A cultural mountain had eroded, but as it was washed away the remnant bedrock of Calum MacLeod's road appeared as haunting and precious as fossilised foot-

prints on any other distant shore. Television pro-
grammes lingered over it. A strathspey in D major
was written about it by a member of the popular band
Capercaillie. In the early summer of 2004 an exhibi-
tion of art entitled 'Calum's Road' was mounted in the
Skye gallery An Tuireann. It featured pottery created
by Patricia Shone, who, according to one critic, 'took
clay over to Raasay and pressed it on to the tracks of
the famous road, which resulted in beautifully textured
jars with uneven edges and peaty colours, which I
could not resist touching'.

Calum's road started to feature – in prose that was
either breathless or brutally factual – in the guide-
books. 'Those who make it to the north of the
island', reads one such entry, 'may wish to note that
the two miles of road linking Brochel to Arnish were
the work of one man, Calum MacLeod. He decided
to build the road himself after the council turned
down his requests for proper access to his home. He
spent between 10 and 15 years building it with the
aid of a pick, a shovel, a wheelbarrow and a road-
making manual which cost him three shillings. He
died in 1988, soon after its completion, and to this
day it is known as "Calum's Road".' It has been
described as a wonder of the modern world. There
has been mention made in the twenty-first century of
applying to UNESCO to have Calum's road recog-
nised as a World Heritage Site.

There were many disputes between councils and
communities concerning access roads in the Highlands

*and Islands in the twentieth century, and there doubt-
less will be more in the twenty-first. Why, then, has
Calum's road become such an enduring parable? Why
not Rhenigidale in Harris or Drinan in Skye? Why not
all of the arterial routes of South Uist or the road to
Applecross in Wester Ross? The answers are elemen-
tary. The first is that Calum MacLeod's community
was the smallest of the small, the most neglected of the
neglected; it was located on the furthermost point of
one of the least prominent of the lonely Hebrides. And
the second is, of course, that a road was finally built to
Arnish not by the council, or the Department of
Agriculture, or the Royal Engineers, and not even
by a community, but by one extraordinary man.*

*There is clearly a risk – if 'risk' it is – of sentimen-
talising a definitively robust and unsentimental story. I
am not immune to such things, but, luckily, the story
itself seems to be. The metaphor, the parable of
Calum's road, inspires flights of fancy. The evident
engineering, the solid rock and tarmacadam of
Calum's road inspires a mostly bewildered but deep
and lasting respect. Whatever else is said and written
about this subject, the least firmly grounded of visitors
to Arnish will leave with one essential, important
conclusion: that here lived a man who desired not
fame and money, nor television and radio programmes, nor medals and recognition by UNESCO,
nor paragraphs in travel guides, nor tributes in maga-
zines and newspapers and books; a man who would
have been astonished and bewildered by the tribute of*

an exhibition of art. Calum did not even want a driving licence. He merely wanted a road.

As I hope the dedication of this book makes clear, I owe thanks to many people. I am especially grateful, for their time, experience and expertise, to those former residents of Arnish and Torran Julia MacLeod Allan, Charles MacLeod, Jessie Nicolson and John Nicolson. A number of council and library officials were helpful beyond the call of duty, particularly Gordon Fyfe, Fiona MacLeod and Sam MacNaughton in Inverness, and Alison Beaton, Carol Campbell, David MacClymont, John Macdonald and Moreen Pringle in Skye. Ian MacDonald of the Gaelic Books Council was instructive on the subject of Calum MacLeod's writing. Kirsty Crawford at the BBC archives in Glasgow tirelessly excavated distant radio and television programmes. Lorna Hunter of the Northern Lighthouse Board and Chris Henry of the Northern Lighthouse Museum directed an arc-light on the history of the manned lighthouse in Rona. The recollections and corrections of John Cumming, Gina Ferguson, John Ferguson, Donald Malcolm MacLeod and Alistair Nicolson, all from Raasay, were invaluable. Houston Brown, Cailean Maclean and John Norman MacLeod assisted this project with characteristic enthusiasm. Norma MacLeod freely offered essential advice and information. The personnel and facilities at the archive libraries in Stornoway, Portree and Inverness, and at the National Record Office in

Edinburgh, were as accommodating as ever. My agent, Stan, was a pillar of strength, and Hugh Andrew and his team at Birlinn were supportive to a fault. And, once more, the extraordinary patience and skill of Joan MacIntyre made the researching of this book more of a pleasure than I had any right to expect. All errors and omissions are mine, not theirs. Moran taing.

Roger Hutchinson
Isle of Raasay, 2006

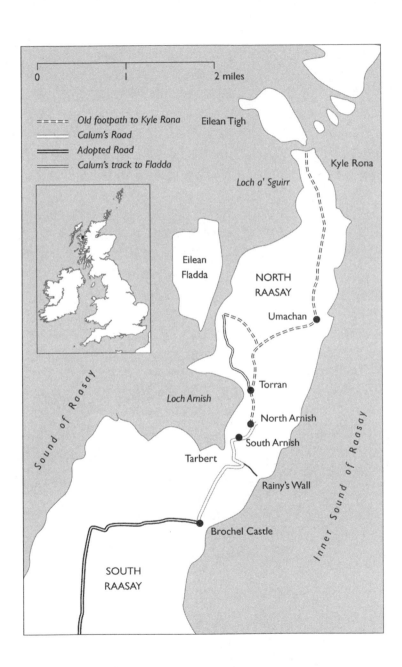

0   1   2 miles

- - - - -   *Old footpath to Kyle Rona*   Eilean Tigh
———   *Calum's Road*
———   *Adopted Road*
———   *Calum's track to Fladda*

Kyle Rona

Loch a' Sguirr

Eilean
Fladda

NORTH
RAASAY

Umachan

Loch Arnish

Torran

North Arnish

South Arnish

Tarbert

Rainy's Wall

Brochel Castle

Sound of Raasay

Inner Sound of Raasay

SOUTH
RAASAY

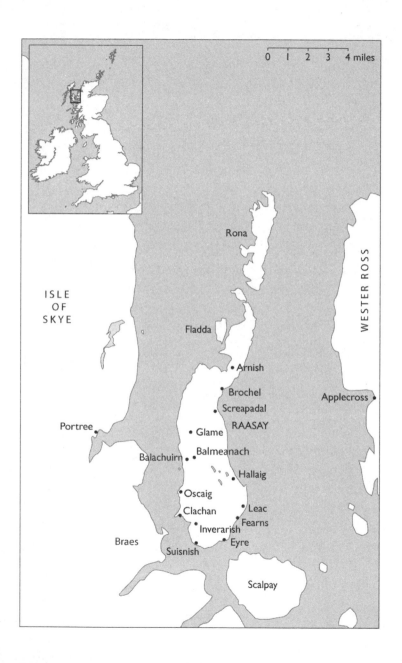

0 1 2 3 4 miles

Rona

WESTER ROSS

ISLE
OF
SKYE

Fladda

• Arnish

Brochel

Screapadal

RAASAY

Applecross •

Portree

• Glame

Balmeanach

Balachuirn

Hallaig

• Oscaig

Clachan

Leac

Fearns

Inverarish

Braes

Eyre

Suisnish

Scalpay

The Island of Strong Men

There are indeed no roads through the island, unless a few detached beaten tracks deserve that name.

James Boswell, *Journal of a Tour to the Hebrides*, 1773

On a spring morning in the middle of the 1960s a man in his fifties placed into his homemade wooden wheelbarrow a pick, an axe, a shovel and a lunchbox. He trundled this cargo south from his crofthouse door, down a familiar, narrow, rutted bridle path, up and down rough Hebridean hillsides, along the edge of hazardous cliff-faces, through patches of bent and stunted hazel and birch and over quaking peat bogs.

After almost two miles he stopped and turned to face homewards. Before him and to his left were steep banks of bracken, turf, birch and hazel. To his right, green pastureland rolled down to the sea. There were sheep on this pasture, and, close to the shore, a small group of waist-high stone rectangles which once, a century ago, had been the thatched cottages of a community called Castle. The vestigial masonry of a medieval keep teetered on an outstanding crag a few yards from the deserted homesteads, melding into the bedrock so naturally that, 500 years after they were first erected and 300 years since they were last occupied, it had become difficult to tell from a hundred yards away where the remnant walls of the man-made fortress finished and the natural stone began.

Then, alone in an empty landscape, he began to build a road.

He started by widening his workspace. He cleared the scattered clumps of wind-blasted native woodland which lay on either side of the old track. He chopped the dwarf trees down, and then he dug up their roots. He gathered the detritus carefully into piles at the edge of his planned route. He worked a long day. He was accustomed to working long days.

And at the end of that first long day, when he re-assembled his equipment in the wheelbarrow and began his walk home, he had denuded several yards of ground. He had, in fact, accomplished slightly more than one-thousandth of a task which would take him twenty years to complete, which would pay him not a material penny and would cost him little more, but which would leave his manifesto marked in stone upon his people's land.

His name was Calum MacLeod. He belonged to the township of South Arnish in the north of the island of Raasay.

*　　*　　*

This story is set in a very small place. On the North Atlantic rim of Europe, off the north-western seaboard of Scotland, lies a group of islands known as the Hebrides. There are several hundred Hebrides. None of them is very big, and none of them, in a global context, has ever been home to a great number of people. But almost all of these islands have at one time or another given shelter, hearth and home to somebody, somebody who could find a way of surviving and even thriving through eight months of winter and sixteen weeks of indifferent maritime weather.

The larger Hebrides are comparatively well known. They include Lewis, with its twenty-first-century population of 20,000 people, Mull and – for many the most resonant and celebrated of all – the rugged, sub-Alpine island of Skye.

Skye lies close to the littoral of the mainland Scottish Highlands. In several places a very strong mythological Celtic hero could have thrown a stone from Skye to Scotland, or taken a decent run-up and long-jumped over the Kyle of Lochalsh. But as the fingers of Skye grope further north and west, towards the island's cousins in the Outer Hebrides, they move away from the hills and sheltered glens of Wester Ross and out into a troubled sea.

If Skye is thought of as somebody's left hand, laid open, as if to be read, with fingers splayed, then the thumb and what palmists call the Mount of Venus in the south and west – which for convenience we will name the district of Sleat and Strath – lie nearest to the mainland. But our attention is drawn to the little finger straining towards the north and the chopping edge of the hand below it, facing the east.

These are the Skye districts of Trotternish and Braes, which are punctuated by the deep central harbour of market town and administrative centre, Portree. Under different geological circumstances the people of Trotternish, Portree and Braes would, in decent weather, enjoy an uninterrupted view across eleven miles of sea to the stark hills of Applecross on the western mainland.

They do not have this view because the archipelago of Raasay, Rona, Fladda and Eilean Tighe obscure it. Raasay, at twelve miles in length and two to three miles in width, is by far the largest of the four. Eilean Tighe, at about half a square mile, is the smallest. This raggedly beautiful quartet sits like a flotilla of small craft at anchor between the west coast of Scotland and the east coast of Skye.

From the looming coastlines of Skye and Applecross they can, to the uninformed eye, appear to be one land mass, so narrow and angular are the channels between them. The greatest bulk by far of this insular group is formed by the hills, grazings and meadows of central and southern Raasay. Those thirty square miles, to pursue our anatomical analogy, emerge from the sea like a muscular forearm.

But in their northern extremes the muscles wither and contract, and Raasay itself thins out into no more than a crooked finger of land, beckoning the northern sea. Upon this arthritic peninsula, around two wide bays known as Loch Arnish and Loch a' Sguirr, stand a handful of old townships. To the west of the peninsula, accessible by foot over slippery rocks and seaweed at low tide, sits the small but relatively fertile island of Fladda. To the north of the finger, like an extra, disconnected joint, is the even smaller island of Eilean Tighe. And to the north of both Eilean Tighe and Raasay, at the other side of half a mile of treacherous sea, is Rona – Ronaidh, the island of seals – stony Rona, with its deep natural harbours, its caves and its arid dusting of soil. There are trees – stunted and bent, but still trees – on the northern finger of Raasay. There is pasture and even arable land on Fladda. There are neither worth mentioning on the four thin miles of Rona.

This group is the Hebrides in tiniest microcosm. The northernmost peninsula of Raasay and the islands of Fladda, Eilean Tighe and Rona are placid, seductive and immeasurably beautiful. Their physical attractions seem almost to influence perceptions of their weather, offering a curiously subjective microclimate to their indulgent inhabitants. When he was sixty-nine years old, and had lived for all but the first couple of those years in this Eden, Calum MacLeod of South Arnish would reflect with the practised eloquence of an ageing infatuate that 'There is bad weather right enough. But the way Raasay is situated it's as though it was sheltered by the island of Skye. For all the world it looks as if the island of Skye was sheltering Raasay in its arms. The high mountains of Skye, you see, they break the course of the Atlantic storms, and we don't have them here.'

Storms or no storms, the islands of Calum MacLeod are so breathtaking that both Trotternish and Wester Ross welcome their interruption of the view. They are littered with the shards of broken hearts. And many of those hearts belong to people who have tried to live there.

Like all of the Hebrides, like all of the Scottish Highlands, these small islands are drenched in a history which has left its mark on every stone, every burn and every clump of birch. But, for obvious and practical reasons, most of the human history of Raasay and its satellites is to be found in the comparatively fertile central and southern districts of the largest island. Between prehistoric times and the nineteenth century, very few people lived in Rona, Fladda and Eilean Tighe – 'tigh' in Gaelic is the singular noun for a house – and only a handful of families occupied the northern Raasay townships of Torran, Arnish, Umachan and Kyle Rona.

Their circumstances have altered little through the centuries. When the educated young Skyeman Martin Martin gathered material for *A Description of the Western Isles of Scotland* in the 1690s he said of Rona – almost certainly from local hearsay rather than personal experience – that 'this little isle is the most unequal rocky piece of Ground to be seen anywhere; there's but very few Acres fit for digging; the whole is covered with long Heath'. Fladda, on the other hand, was 'all plain arable Ground' albeit only 'about a Mile in Circumference' – Fladda is almond shaped, measuring roughly a mile and a third in length and two-thirds of a mile in breadth.

Eighty years later, when the English philosopher Samuel Johnson visited as a guest of the hereditary proprietor John MacLeod in 1773 he noted that 'Raasay is the only inhabited island' in the group. 'Rona and Fladda afford only pasture for cattle, of which one hundred and sixty winter in Rona, under the superintendence of a solitary herdsman.'

Johnson's companion, the Scottish Lowland lawyer and diarist James Boswell, considered that 'The north end of Rasay is as rocky as the south end. From it I saw the little isle of Fladda, belonging to Rasay, all fine green ground;– and Rona, which is of so rocky a soil that it appears to be a pavement.'

That our story is located in those distant and unpromising parts is thanks, chiefly, to a squalid episode in European history.

Samuel Johnson computed the 1773 population of Raasay to be between 600 and 900, which was almost certainly optimistic. Most other visitors and surveyors of the late eighteenth century suggest that 500 or 600 people lived there. He was also possibly wrong in maintaining that Rona was virtually uninhabited. An enumeration made by Church of Scotland ministers in 1764 – just nine years before the visit of Johnson and Boswell – declared that 36 people lived in Rona.

But it is certain that, other than those few ghostly and uncertain families eking out a living on the 'pavement' of Rona, in the last half of the nineteenth century effectively all of the archipelago's inhabitants lived in Raasay, and most of them were settled in the centre and the south of that main island.

And it is equally certain that, within a tiny margin of possible error, fifty years later, in 1841, when a detailed official census was taken, 987 people lived in Raasay, 110 in Rona and 29 in Fladda. A dramatic population swing had started. A further fifty years after that, in 1891, when another national census was taken, the population of Raasay had fallen to 430, while the number of people living in Rona and Fladda had risen to 181 and 51 respectively, and there was a family of 8 living in the tidal outcrop of Eilean Tighe.

In the same period the populations of townships in central and southern Raasay disappeared. In 1861 there were 33 people in Holoman, on the central west coast. By 1891 there were just 5. In the same three decades the population of nearby Balachuirn fell from 49 to 26. In 1841 there were 30 people in the southern township of Eyre. Ten years later, in 1851, there were none.

In 1851, 233 people lived in North and South Fearns on the southern east coast of Raasay. Thirty years later, in 1881, nobody lived there. Leac, a mile along the east coast from Fearns, had a population of 70 in 1841, and was entirely depopulated in 1861.

Perhaps the most emblematic of all these vanishing

Raasay civilisations, thanks to an eponymous epic elegy written in 1954 by the Raasay-born poet Sorley Maclean, was to be found another mile up the coast from Leac. John MacCulloch, who sailed past the townships of Upper and Lower Hallaig early in the nineteenth century, described 'the green and cultivated land . . . on the tops of the high eastern cliffs, which are everywhere covered with farms, that form a striking contrast to the solitary brown waste of the western coast.'

In 1833 the people of Hallaig petitioned the Gaelic Schools Society in Edinburgh for some educational provision, insisting that 'no less than 60 Scholars could be got to attend School'. In the census of 1841 the population of Upper and Lower Hallaig was enumerated to be 129 souls. Then came the eviction notices. By 1861 this busy place had been reduced to a shepherd and a labourer. By the time of the national census for 1891 the returns from Hallaig in Raasay amounted to one eloquent word: 'Nil'.

And up the coast from the two Hallaigs lay North and South Screapadal, whose populations fell from 101 in 1841 to an official 'Nil' in 1861. And there were others, all of the others: Brae, Inver and Glame; Doiredomhain, two miles across the island from Screapadal, whose two families comprising 11 people in 1851 had gone by 1861; Manish, at the north-western shoulder of central Raasay, whose 41 people in 1841 had entirely disappeared within twenty years; and Castle, the community beneath the ruined medieval keep of Brochel, at the join between the strong arm of central Raasay and the crooked finger bending north to Arnish, Torran, Fladda and Rona.*

And the cause of this depopulation? Central and southern Raasay, the bulwark and the foodstore of the population of this island group since the Stone Age, was, between the middle of the nineteenth century and the beginning of the twentieth, turned into a sheep run. Perhaps 500 or 600 people, perhaps half of the population, were evicted by force from Raasay in that period, or by the relentless attrition of unnecessary poverty. Some were transported to Skye, some to Australia, some to Canada, and others to unrecorded corners of the earth.

But some – a minority, but a substantial minority – stayed in the archipelago. We have seen how many of them moved to the formerly uninhabitable islets of Fladda, Rona and Eilean Tighe. Others moved to Torran, Arnish, Umachan and Kyle Rona. That thin, bent and lonely finger of land and its offshore islands had changed, in fifty short years, from an ill-considered outpost to the last redoubt of the native people of the small archipelago which lay between Skye and Wester Ross.

It was not an entirely stricken province. The inhabitants had not been sent to the deserts of Judea. There

---

* Castle was where the road stopped. Castle was where Calum MacLeod set out to remedy that omission in the 1960s. Castle's population fell from 69 in 1841 to 14 in 1891, and never recovered.

were both grazing and arable land in northern Raasay, as well as in Fladda and Eilean Tighe, there was summer grazing in the heather on the hills, and the surrounding sea was teeming with fish. But it was a district which had developed naturally over the centuries a certain, small, sustainable population, and which could not easily absorb more.

The mass eviction of Highland tenants by their nineteenth-century speculating landlords, eager to use their property to farm wool or breed deer, which led to the vacuuming of the human population of southern Raasay and the overcrowding of northern Raasay, Rona, Fladda and Eilean Tighe, was not of course confined to those four islands. It took place over a period of decades across all of the north and west of Scotland, and has come to be known as the Highland Clearances.

It brought in its wake a protracted period of social unrest throughout the area, which frequently sparked into militant action and violent clashes between land-hungry crofters, landless cottars, and those bodies of the law which were called upon by landowning interests to enforce their right to turn ancestral common grazings and arable land into private sheep runs or parks in which to hunt deer.

Many a government would have chosen to sit out the storm and let the cycle of skirmish and arrest continue. William Gladstone's Liberal administration did not. In March 1883 Gladstone's home secretary, Sir William Harcourt, announced that he was setting up a Royal Commission 'to inquire into the conditions of the crofters and cottars in the Highlands and Islands of Scotland'.

The commission moved quickly. It held its first public hearing just two months later, on Tuesday 8 May, at Ollach Church – which was temporarily being used as a schoolroom – in Braes, in Skye, a mile across the sea from southern Raasay. Over the next five months the commission would travel from school-house to drill hall to church premises, from Argyll to Shetland, Lewis and Caithness, meeting in 61 different places and hearing evidence – frequently through a translator of Gaelic – from 775 witnesses.

But in that first month of May it occupied itself in Skye and Raasay. The Raasay hearings of the Royal Commission of Inquiry into the Condition of Crofters and Cottars in the Highlands and Islands took place on Tuesday 22 May at Torran Schoolhouse in the north of the island. This choice of venue was significant. Any such public meeting held half a century earlier would certainly have been staged in the south of Raasay – at Fearns, perhaps, or Hallaig – because that was where most of the people lived. By 1883 it was not even plausible to hold a meeting at each end of Raasay. Apart from the estate village close to Raasay House at Clachan, and a handful of herdsmen and shepherds and Home Farm labourers, and an even smaller handful of residual southern crofters scattered around the rest of the island, none of the archipelago's population of 700 lived in the south. Torran Schoolhouse was therefore formally acknowledged by the British Government, for the first and perhaps the last time in history, as the centre of the archipelago's community.

The commissioners had been meeting on the previous day at the Free Church in Glendale, a celebrated centre of rebellion close to Dunvegan on the northwest coast of Skye. They travelled to Raasay on Monday evening aboard HMS *Lively*, a substantial steam- and sail-driven despatch boat whose last notable engagement had involved transporting famine-relief supplies to Ireland two years earlier, and who was to be at the commissioners' call until she hit a rock and foundered fatally off the coast of Lewis in June.

On the night of 21 May the *Lively* left Loch Dunvegan and made safe landfall off northern Raasay, putting down anchor in Loch Arnish. The commissioners ate and slept aboard, and were rowed ashore in the morning to walk the short distance up a steep coastal track to Torran Schoolhouse. 'The coast scenery here is of a grand description', reported a correspondent to the *Scotsman* newspaper later that day. 'The shores of Loch Arnish are exceedingly striking, especially at the upper end where the steep banks for a good way up are clad with small birch trees, forming a pretty coppice above which rise bold granite crags. The proceedings took place at the School House at Torran, which is built on a picturesque site among the birches under the cliffs, and near it are several crofter's houses, with little patches of cultivated ground on the face of rocks, to which it might be thought even goats would have difficulty in clambering.'

The members of the Royal Commission who arrived at this pretty place on 22 May 1883 were a mixture of the landed aristocracy and the Highland professional classes. They were chaired by the man who would give the commission its name: Francis, 9th Lord Napier and 1st Baron Ettrick, a 64-year-old Lowland Scottish professional diplomat and colonial administrator who had briefly been viceroy of India. Napier had been given an interesting committee. It consisted of two out-and-out representatives of the Highland land-owning interest – the Inverness-shire Tory MP Donald Cameron of Lochiel and Sir Kenneth Mackenzie of Gairloch – and three others.

The latter three were all Gaelic speakers, and they all possessed to one degree or another sympathy with and knowledge of the crofters' case. They were the radical MP for Inverness Burghs, Charles Fraser-Mackintosh; Alexander Nicolson, who was at the time sheriff of Kircudbright but who came from Skye (Sgurr Alasdair in the black heart of that island's Cuillin mountain range is named after his pioneering ascent); and Professor Donald MacKinnon from the island of Colonsay, the first occupant of the Chair of Celtic at Edinburgh University. Another Colonsay man – and another Gaelic speaker – Malcolm Mac-Neill, was appointed secretary to the commission. These seven eminences trooped up through the birch groves to Torran Schoolhouse, entered and took their seats at the head of the room before a packed assembly.

The first witness to be called was sixty-year-old Charles MacLeod, a crofter and fisherman of the neighbouring township of Arnish. Charles MacLeod, he affirmed to Lord Napier, had been 'freely elected' as the delegate of Arnish by the male heads of its five different families, who in 1883 numbered between them around thirty people. Charles had a family of his own. He had a daughter named Kate, who would marry a man from Arnish named Malcolm MacLeod. In 1882, the year before the Napier Commission hearings, this couple had borne a son and christened him Donald. Donald MacLeod would in his turn father a son named Calum, who a hundred years later would still be living in Arnish, and who we recently left by his wheelbarrow in the middle of the 1960s, beginning to build a road.

It appears that certain skills and qualities were passed down from great-grandfather to great-grandson. Eloquence was one of them. 'It is with the view of getting deliverance from bondage into liberty', Charles MacLeod told the Napier Commission, 'that we have come out here today. We would take the example from those who were in bondage, and who were sighing in their bondage, and wishing for liberty. The Israelites before were in bondage, but there was One above who heard the sighing of those in bondage, and fixed the time for coming for their deliverance.

'We are oppressed with cultivating bad land, which yields no crop, which does not return to us the value of our work. There are many reasons for that, the way the island is circumstanced. In days gone by this island was called the island of the big men – the island of strong men – and it deserved that name. From the days of John MacGillicallum of Raasay, it was rearing able men, until within the last few generations. They would defend their islands and the islands about. They were raising fighting men in this island to defend their own homestead and the kingdom.

'And now, what has caused the people of this island to come down to their present condition? I remember from the time of my father, they were raising their families. My father reared five sons, and now the land which my father had is occupied by three families; two of them are occupying the land which my father had, and each of their families is as heavy as my father's family was. They have no more arable land [between them] as my father had.'

With his carefully prepared statement concluded, Charles MacLeod then answered precise questions from Francis, Lord Napier, which confirmed that he personally had two cows and their calves, eight sheep, no horse, and a few 'spots here and there' of potatoes and oats. Charles Fraser-Mackintosh, the MP who at a general election two years later would resign his comfortable urban seat of Inverness Burghs and, as a 'Crofters' Candidate' in the constituency of rural Inverness-shire, defeat his fellow tribune on the Napier Commission, Cameron of Lochiel, took up the questioning.

'With regard to the depopulation of the island in former times,' asked Fraser-Mackintosh, 'was not Raasay at one time full of people?'

'Yes,' said Charles MacLeod.

'When did the people first begin to be put out of the island?'

'It is forty years since the first removings.'

'You complain you have not enough land to work?'

'Yes.'

'Where could you or your co-crofters get land?'

'On the property of the island.'

'Where?'

'In the townships which are waste.'

'In whose possession are they?'

'Under sheep belonging to the proprietor.'

'Is there any big tenant [sheep-farmer]?'

'There was a farmer named Mackenzie there a few years ago.'

'Who has got that farm now?'

'The proprietor has got it.'

'Has he a great deal in his own hands under sheep?'

'Yes.'

'Has he all that Mackenzie had?'

'Yes.'

Charles Fraser-Mackintosh and Charles MacLeod had, within an hour of the hearing's commencement, reached the nub of the matter. The first clearances of the southern bulk of Raasay had indeed, as we have seen from the census statistics, begun about 'forty years since', in the late 1830s and early 1840s. They were carried out during the supremacy of the last hereditary clan chief, John MacLeod of Raasay.

An officer in the 78th Highlanders, John MacLeod

was largely absent from his island domain. He was the grandson of the John MacLeod who had entertained Samuel Johnson and James Boswell, and he inherited the substantial debts which had been incurred by his grandfather's extravagant investments in such amenities as the large mansion house in which – while the wind howled outside – Johnson had found 'plenty and elegance, beauty and gaiety'.

In a desperate attempt to fend off his creditors, young John MacLeod instructed his factor to evict their people from such places as Eyre, Suisnish and Upper Hallaig and to let the cleared land as profitable sheep farms to 'tacksmen', or tenant farmers. It was to no avail. The creditors foreclosed in the early 1840s, and in 1843 John MacLeod of Raasay abdicated and emigrated. Three years later his family estate was sold, by trustees acting on behalf of the creditors, to a wealthy merchant trader named George Rainy.

Rainy pursued his predecessor's domestic policies. He was also anxious to prevent those who managed to remain even on the outer edges of his new estate from multiplying by natural means. As Donald MacLeod of Kyle Rona would tell the Napier Commission at Torran Schoolhouse in 1883, 'Mr Rainy enacted a rule that no-one should marry on the island. There was one man there who married in spite of him, and because he did he [Rainy] put him out of his father's house and that man went to a bothy, to a sheep cot. Mr Rainy then came and demolished the sheep cot upon him and extinguished his fire and neither friend nor anyone else dared to give him a night's shelter. He was not allowed entrance into any house.'

This particular persecution occurred in 1850. Before torching it, Rainy's evictors had carried a baby in a cradle out of the building. The surname of the baby was MacLeod, and the scene of the outrage was North Arnish.

In that same year, the fourth of his ascendancy, George Rainy amalgamated the privatised tacks, or farmland, of Suisnish and Eyre with those of Glen and Glame and Brae and let them as one big lot to a sheep-farmer from Assynt in the mainland Highlands named Royston MacKenzie. This 'farmer named Mackenzie' of Charles MacLeod's testimony was an ambitious man. Within two years his sheep were running across almost all of the denuded west side of Raasay. By 1854 MacKenzie had the east side too. Within four or five years of Mr Royston and Mrs Hughina MacKenzie arriving from Assynt to set up house in an otherwise empty Suisnish, Royston's sheep grazed across the whole of Raasay south of Loch Arnish, excepting the Home Farm, some other small estate properties and a handful of residual crofts.

The new regime therefore consisted of two elements. George Rainy had a Georgian mansion house and walled garden, a Home Farm, an elegant harbour in Clachan Bay and a fishing and shooting estate stocked with trout, deer, rabbits and pheasant, as well as, fortuitously, seals, otters and golden eagles, all of which were bagged with merriment – inedible seals

and otters were regarded as useful target practice;
equally inedible eagles were stuffed and preserved in
glass boxes. The deer and rabbits shared most of the
island with Royston MacKenzie's thousands of sheep,
which – unlike the unfortunate eagles, seals and otters
– were not considered fair game.

   Almost everybody who was not directly employed
by either of those two interests was obliged to live,
preferably without reproducing, north of Loch Arnish.
This arrangement was formalised by the creation
during the Rainy supremacy of a 'deer fence' – actually
a forbidding six-foot-high dry-stone wall – which was
erected across the narrowest point of Raasay, halfway
between Castle and Arnish, through a mile-long glen
from the east coast to the west, where it ran down to
the waters of south Loch Arnish. Its incidental pre-
vention of access to a traditional anchorage named
Port an Altainn was like the sort of arbitrary insult
which might be thrown after an extremely serious
injury. Local men were hired to build the wall. They
were paid in kind, receiving a stone of meal in return
for each week's labour. Their foreman was given £8
sterling to oversee the whole project.*

---

* In 1989 John 'London' Nicolson of Torran recalled how, at the
age of seven in 1942, he had first encountered the vividly symbolic 'Rainy's Wall'. 'I had not seen such a high fence before', he
wrote, 'and it was so well made compared with the fences in
Torran and Arnish: talk about the Berlin Wall! Little did I
appreciate that the fence had been placed there to keep people
off "game ground" rather than to stop game from creating havoc
in crofters' "cabbage patches".'

In the limited landscape north of this barrier men and women could live and graze their animals and attempt to grow crops, in return for an annual rental whose default would result in swift eviction. In the fat forearm of Raasay to its south were sheep, deer, rabbits and more sheep. The crofters' stock was not, of course, permitted to graze south of the fence. But, in contrast to the proprietor's tenantry, the proprietor's game was encouraged to proliferate in the groves, heather and scrubland north of it. Tenants were never, ever allowed to kill pheasant or deer. The question was moot as to whether crofters were permitted to shoot the few rabbits they were able to catch in the act of eating the vegetables growing on their rented lots. Most thought that they were not so permitted, some thought that they were. When asked in 1883 by the Napier Commission, 'So far as a man killed rabbits on his own croft, would he be scolded or molested?' the estate factor said, 'That is a hard question. He might get scolded.'

In 1863 George Rainy died, leaving the estate to his son, George Haygarth Rainy. In 1872 George Haygarth Rainy died and the estate was bought by George G. MacKay. MacKay only had the place for two years, during which time he managed to strip the six remaining crofters at Balachuirn in central Raasay of their land and increase the annual rentals of crofters in, for instance, Arnish, by as much as 73 per cent, and in Fladda from a total of £22 to £30 per annum.

In 1874 William James Armitage of Southgate in

London bought out George G. MacKay. Armitage
spent one summer in his Hebridean fiefdom, and then
sold it in 1876 to the 25-year-old Edward Herbert
Wood, the heir to a Staffordshire Five Towns' pottery
fortune. Edward Herbert Wood was more interested in
shooting than sheep, and was not short of money.
Luckily for Wood, Royston MacKenzie had died in
1873. He reclaimed the sheep farm, reduced the stock
by half, from 3,200 to about 1,600, and replaced them
on the hills and grazings with deer.

'Would you be satisfied if you got more hill pasture?' Charles Fraser-Mackintosh asked Charles
MacLeod in 1883.

'We would try to put up with it,' said Charles
MacLeod, meaning that it would be better than nothing. 'Our lots are spoiled with game, pheasants and
rabbits, so much so that it is not worth our while
sowing our ground at all.'

'Have you remonstrated against that to Mr Wood?'

'Yes.'

'What relief has he given you?'

'We got no relief, and the feeding boxes for the
pheasants are placed at the end of our arable ground.'

'Have you liberty to kill rabbits or to trap them?'

'No.'

'You mentioned something about a deer fence,' said
Sir Kenneth MacKenzie to Charles MacLeod shortly
afterwards. 'Is there a deer fence cutting you off from
the proprietor's lands?'

'Yes.'

'Is it a matter of complaint that that fence should be there?'

'It is a cause of complaint, for our cattle cannot get to our own pasturage, owing to the roughness of the ground leading to it, and the fence is in the way. They are shut in in their own hill pasture by this fence.'

Forgivably, Sir Kenneth did not quite understand the minutiae of this concern about access. 'Have they their own hill pasture behind this fence?'

'No.'

'You would like to cross part of the proprietor's land to get to a remote part of your own pasture?'

'The fence was fixed so close to rocky ground that our cows cannot get between these rocks and their own ground to their pasturage.'

'If the line of fence was altered, would that satisfy you?'

'That is what we were wishing to be done,' said Calum MacLeod's great-grandfather. 'To have it put back for a few yards. We were wanting this when the fence was put up.'

Then, perhaps hurriedly, possibly aware of so much remaining to be said, so many greater issues still undeclared, so much left to be understood, he added, as if suddenly reminded of it, 'There is no port for hauling up our boats on our ground.'

Charles MacLeod was thanked by Lord Napier, and sat down.

Murdo Nicolson, a 48-year-old crofter and fisher-man of Torran itself – one of the tenants of those 'little patches of cultivated ground on the face of rocks' observed by the *Scotsman*'s correspondent – followed Charles MacLeod to the witness stand.

Murdo Nicolson had moved to Torran ten years earlier from Fladda, where his father had a croft and where Murdo had been raised. He travelled seasonally to work on the east-coast herring fleets, and fished locally out of a fifteen-foot boat for herring and lobster. He wished simply, he said, 'for a better place'. Asked by Lord Napier if he and his neighbours supported themselves chiefly by fishing, he said, 'They do their utmost at the fishing, but it will give them enough to do to support themselves by fishing.'

And the land was little easier. 'There is such an amount of scrub bush growing on our crofts,' Murdo Nicolson told Charles Fraser-Mackintosh, 'and we are not allowed to cut it, and we are prevented by it from cultivating our crofts.'

'Would you like to see all this pretty wood here about cut down?'

'The wood is not so pretty as that.'

'Is it not useful sometimes for different purposes to have a little bit of wood?'

'No, it is a source of loss to us every day of the year. The game shelter in the wood and spoil our crop, and we get nothing for it.'

'Is your land good enough to grow heavy crops if there were no game?' asked Cameron of Lochiel.

'There is no doubt it would be considerably better were it not for the game,' said Murdo Nicolson. 'It is only bad ground at all events. I believe it is as bad as is to be found between the two ends of Raasay.'

'I suppose', said Cameron of Lochiel, 'the game don't do any harm to the potatoes?'

'The pheasants and rabbits spoil the potatoes on us.'

'Do rabbits eat potatoes?'

'Yes, they do that indeed.'

Once Cameron of Lochiel's lesson in the diet of rabbits was concluded, the commission heard from John Gillies, a fifty-year-old crofter and fisherman who had been elected to represent the fifty-four people of Fladda. He and his neighbours, he said, 'are complaining, as others are, about the hardness of the land, and the dearness of it. It is dear, it is bad, and there is little of it.'

There was another grievance, unique to the tidal island of Fladda. 'They are also wanting to speak about the channel between them and the island,' said John Gillies. 'They come from the island to the school here [in Torran], and the channel is not wider than thirty yards at high tide. Sometimes the children are starving waiting for the tide, when they cannot get over – when the men are away from home [and their boats unavailable].'

'You mean coming back from school?' asked Lord Napier.

'Yes; but many days they cannot go to school at all.'

'How wide is the channel at high water?'

'Thirty yards, and it is dry at half tide.'

'What remedy do you suggest for this?'

'Either to bridge the channel, or to give us another place to live in, from which our children could go to school in safety.'

'Would it be easy to bridge the channel?'

'It would not be difficult at all. There are plenty of materials – plenty of stones thereabout.'

Kyle Rona was the northernmost community in Raasay itself, another mile and a half up the coast from Umachan and eponymously situated on the southern shore of the Kyle of Rona. The ten heads of family in its overburdened community had in 1883 elected a 78-year-old retired fisherman named Donald MacLeod to be their delegate to the Napier Commission.

'I have only to say', said Donald MacLeod, 'what the rest have said, that it is poverty sent me here – that I am situated on bad ground, and little of it, and too dear, and that for a long time. In my own memory it was five families who were in the township numbering twenty-nine individuals, and today there are ten families and eighty.'

'We want to find out', said Charles Fraser-Mackintosh to this Raasay man who had been born in around 1805, and who had lived all his days in Kyle Rona, 'if you know about the evictions in former times. The first one began in the time of MacLeod himself about forty years ago. Do you recollect that?'

'I don't remember the first removing, but I remember Mr Rainy about thirty years ago clearing fourteen townships, and he made them into a sheep farm which he had in his own hands.'

'What became of the people?'

'They went to other kingdoms – some to America, some to Australia, and to other places that they could think of.'

'Will you give us a rough estimate of the population of the fourteen townships?'

'I cannot; there were a great number of people.'

'Were they hundreds?'

'Yes, hundreds, young and old. I am sure there were about one hundred in each of two townships.'

'Will you name the towns?'

'Castle, Screpidale, two Hallaigs, Ceancnock, Leachd, two Fearns, Eyre, Suisinish, Doirredomhain, Mainish.'

'Was there a good deal of arable land upon these townships?'

'They were altogether arable land capable of being ploughed.'

'Are these now altogether in the proprietor's hands?'

'Yes, indeed. The only occupants of that land today are rabbits and deer and sheep.'

'Did the people out of these fourteen townships that Rainy cleared go of their own accord?'

'No, not at all. The people were very sorry to leave at that time. They were weeping and wailing and lamenting. They were taking handfuls of grass that was growing over the graves of their families in the churchyard, as remembrances of their kindred.'

Lord Napier himself concluded the questioning of Donald MacLeod. 'I have seen in an old book', said the chairman, 'that there was once a large place in the middle of the island here which was free to anybody to take their cattle to in summer – a kind of wild place, for the summer sheilings. Did you ever hear of that?'

'I believe the hill pasture is there yet,' said Donald MacLeod. 'That was the case. If the hill pasture was there, it is not there now for the people.'

If Kyle Rona, Umachan, Fladda, Torran and Arnish had it hard, one place had it harder than them all. The four square miles of Rona were bigger both in acreage and – in 1883 – in population than all of northern Raasay. We have heard already of the legendary in-hospitality of Rona. When the landowner George Rainy was asked in 1851 to describe his new property to a previous investigative body, the MacNeill Commission, he informed Sir John MacNeill that 'the island of Rona . . . is almost entirely composed of masses of bare rock'.

In that same year, 1851, there were, thanks largely to the 'removings' of Rainy's predecessor, the last MacLeod of Raasay, 115 people in Rona. This amounted to at least a quadrupling in half a century. In 1871, the last year of the governance of the small insular group by the Rainy family, the population of this 'mass of bare rock' had been swollen to 157. Ten years later 176 people were housed in desuetude in the island, which historically had been considered by all observers to be, if not completely uninhabited, then effectively uninhabitable. In contrast to the rest of the archipelago, Donald MacLeod of Kyle Rona told the

Napier Commission, nobody had ever been evicted from Rona. This was not an oversight, and it was not mercy. It was because nobody voluntarily lived there. 'The people were not living in Rona at first at all. They were sent to Rona.'

'Should I be here from sunrise to sunset', said 36-year-old John Nicolson of Doire na Guaile in the south of Rona, 'I could not fully disclose the poverty of Rona. It is a place in which no man need expect to make his living. We are working on sea and land, both summer and winter, and spring – every quarter of the year – and after that we have only poverty.'

There followed the familiar litany of overcrowding, of too many people obliged to eke out a livelihood on too little bad land. But although he was still a relatively young man John Nicolson had no desire to emigrate.

'There are more of my friends in America and Australia than there are in Raasay,' he said.

'You don't feel encouraged to go to any of these places?' asked Sheriff Alexander Nicolson.

'No, I would like to have a place in the land of my birth.'

'But is it not a fact that there are men who went from Skye without a penny, who are now members of parliament and rich men in Canada and Australia?'

'I cannot know about that, but I have no mind to go abroad.'

'You would rather stay in Rona, bad as it is, than try your chance in these places?'

'It is likely. I am there for some time past at any rate,

and I am trying sea and land, and every one in the place is in the same way. We have gone to the east coast fishing with our bags to sell ourselves there to the highest bidder, and after all I have known many coming home, and the [east coast] masters could not, after the fishing was over, give them one shilling of their own earnings to bring them home. The fishing is only a lottery.'

That was the situation of the MacLeods of Arnish and their neighbours in Torran, Umachan, Kyle Rona, Fladda, Eilean Tighe and the island of Rona in 1883. They had either been sent north of the deer fence to overpopulate a place that could barely sustain human life, or they were native to that place and had been incrementally, over recent decades, obliged to share their thin ground with scores of the dispossessed of southern Raasay.

They were given no thanks and little or no practical assistance for surviving in this hopeless condition. The people of Fladda were denied a small bridge across thirty yards of sea. The people of southern Rona had no road 'except a track among the rocks and bogs' between themselves and the school and anchorage at Dryharbour. The latest proprietor, Edward Herbert Wood, was comparatively well regarded for employing local men in such initiatives as the construction of a four-mile-long, six-foot-wide cart track, at a cost of £395, between Torran and Kyle Rona.

But, in essence, George Herbert Wood was no more than the last of a quick succession of private landowners, all of whom either passively accepted or actively continued the MacLeod–Rainy policy of depopulating central and southern Raasay, sending as many people as possible overseas, and removing the rest to the rural ghetto north of the deer fence. Edward Herbert Wood showed no inclination to apply an obvious and often-suggested solution to his Aboriginal Question: to permit the hungry and homeless of Rona and northern Raasay to return to the southern arable land and good grazings of their grandparents.

This was because at least one interest had benefited from the 'removings' policy. The landowner himself was presently in possession of an increasingly valuable financial asset. In 1846 George Rainy had paid £27,660 for the estate, almost £1.8 million in today's terms. Just thirty years later, in 1876, Edward Herbert Wood paid £65,000 – equivalent to £4 million today – for exactly the same acreage, and that during a period of national deflation rather than inflation, a time when the purchasing power of the pound sterling had actually increased. In order to maintain or improve the value of the landowner's investment it was clear that the status quo must be maintained, and the status quo by the 1870s and 1880s was that the arable land and grazings of the majority of Raasay was devoted to sheep and game.

The Napier Commission's report did result, three years later, in the reforming Crofters Act of 1886. This gave sitting tenants the right to security of tenure and a fair rental adjudicated by an independent commission.

It was a considerable advance for those who had managed to hang on to a decent croft. But it did little or nothing for those who had little or nothing. It did not put the demographic clock back to 1830. It did not restore their descendants to Hallaig and Fearns. It did not solve the conundrum of Rona, whose population continued to grow. Ten years after Napier, in 1893, yet another Royal Commission would be angrily informed by Alexander Gillies of Kyle Rona that 'I know there is land on the other side of Raasay, of the breadth of the sole of my shoe, which would be almost better than half an acre of the land I have now. It is not soil, but rocks we are occupying.'

But that 'land on the other side of Raasay' was not forthcoming, and as the nineteenth turned into the twentieth century it showed no further signs of being reallocated to the descendants of its original inhabitants. Tired of profitless toil and with no predictable solution to their decennial crisis, those descendants began to leave. Between 1891 and 1921 the population of Rona fell from 181 to 98. In the same period the population of Fladda declined from 51 to 21, and the populations of Kyle Rona, Torran, Umachan and Arnish collapsed by similar degrees.

The missing people did not so much go abroad, this time. They travelled south and east instead, to the jobs and wages promised by the burgeoning heavy industries and trading vessels of Aberdeen, Lothian, England and – more than anywhere else – Clydeside.

Two such emigrants, typical of their time, were Donald MacLeod of Arnish and Julia Gillies of Fladda. Donald, that grandson of the Charles MacLeod who had been the first man to testify before Lord Napier at Torran Schoolhouse in 1883, worked as a merchant seaman out of Glasgow. There, the couple married and appeared to settle. On 15 November 1911 a son was born to them in the city. Donald and Julia christened him Malcolm, after Donald's father, which forename in their Gaelic-speaking household was rendered as Calum.

They might, like so many others, never have returned. But Calum MacLeod was a sickly infant, and within a year or two Donald and Julia were advised to remove him for the sake of his health from the urban fumes. Upon the outbreak of the First World War in 1914 the young MacLeod family returned to the birch trees, scrub, inlets and rough croftland of northern Raasay, to Donald's father's township of South Arnish.

At least, Calum – carefully nursing his father's silver watch, which he would treasure for the rest of his life – and his mother, Julia, returned, to the croft and house adjacent to that of Donald's father. Donald MacLeod himself, by now a quartermaster in the merchant navy, served his country at sea throughout the First World War. It was a period not without incident. 'At one time', his youngest son, Charles, would say, 'the ship he was sailing in was stopped by a submarine off the Spanish coast. The submarine allowed the crew to get off in the boats, and then they put time-bombs in the ship. They didn't waste a torpedo on it, but they allowed the crew to row ashore in Spain – I think it was at Vigo – and they got home from there.' That ship, lost to enemy action in 1917, was the MV *Aislaby* of the Harrowing Steamship Company of Whitby in Yorkshire.

Donald MacLeod would continue to serve beneath the red ensign in peacetime; 'that was his life's work', said Charles MacLeod. 'He kept going away to sea up until about 1930. He only returned permanently shortly after I was born in 1929.' Before Charles's birth and her husband's retirement from the merchant navy, Julia MacLeod raised four children – Calum, his other brother Ronald and their sisters Katie and Bella – on the Arnish croft. Calum had another sister, Bella Dolly, who died in infancy during the 1919 Spanish flu pandemic. 'Donald's wife [Julia] was a most capable crofter's partner', their neighbour John 'London' Nicolson of Torran* would write, 'and with her knowledge of herbs, plants and medicaments, could cure man and beast . . . She looked after the cash and was said to be tight with it. In fairness to her, she knew it was hard-earned and was being careful.'

After moving from the unhealthy urban atmosphere, Calum MacLeod's strength returned. He would

* Two John Nicolsons of Torran, each born and brought up there in the 1920s, have given accounts which will be quoted from in this book. The first and (by a couple of years) the youngest is the one mentioned above. To distinguish him from his cousin, and all other John Nicolsons, he was sometimes given the cognomen John 'London', on account of his long and distinguished service to the Gaelic Society of London. For the same reason he will be referred to as John 'London' in this text. Plain John Nicolson is his slightly older relative.

always thereafter appreciate northern Raasay as the apotheosis of both physical and moral health and vigour, in direct counterpoint to what he perceived as the endemic corruption of urban society. Between the ages of six and fifteen he attended Torran public school, along with thirty-two other scholars from all across north Raasay and Fladda. Their sole instructor at this single-teacher school was a former customs and excise officer from Glendale in Skye named James 'Seumas Ruadh' MacKinnon.

Seumas Ruadh was, even for his time, an idiosyncratic dominie. He was crippled as the result of a childhood accident and could get about only with the help of a walking stick. He was not a strict disciplinarian. In the words of another of his students, 'He must truly have been the forerunner of liberal studies. The children certainly had the benefit of an unfettered outdoor life, and when the older boys felt that there was a tightening up of school discipline, for some mysterious reason the chimney began to have "blowdowns", and this always heralded the end of another school day.' The 'blowdowns' were caused, naturally, not by a swirling and unpredictable wind, but by the artful placing by one of Seumas Ruadh's pupils of a turf on the Torran School chimney pot.

'Mr MacKinnon ran the Post Office as well,' said another pupil. 'It was in the residents' part of the school. When the postman went past the school window with the day's delivery for him to sort, there was great hilarity – with everybody shouting "post", and

Mr MacKinnon went off then to do the post, and of course that's when everybody went haywire – [writing] slates and pencils and everything went flying all over the place.' The Torran School tawse, that painful enforcer of Scottish schoolteachers' authority, was on such occasions tossed up into the building's roof ventilator.

Whether or not Seumas Ruadh MacKinnon was a pioneer of liberal studies, he was certainly a rare early-twentieth-century practitioner of Gaelic Medium Education. Calum MacLeod received most of his schooling in his native language. ' "Ginger James" . . . taught his pupils in Gaelic and had little time for English!' reported one former pupil. MacKinnon's successor, Miss Rita Campbell from Scullamus in south Skye, discovered upon arriving at Torran in 1929 that 'children at the age of ten and over . . . had the barest knowledge of the English language'.

Which might partly be why, at the age of fourteen, in 1925, his last year at Torran or any other school, Calum MacLeod was entered in an annual Gaelic essay competition organised by the Celtic Society of New York.* The influence of 'Ginger James' perhaps

---

* The Celtic Society of New York, or Comunn Gaidhealach New York, was founded in 1892. One of its aims was 'to provide a means by which the members of the society can become better acquainted with their mother tongue in order to speak it precisely and eloquently'. It held monthly Gaelic literacy classes and was the first body in the United States to offer prizes for Gaelic song and recitation. Its annual Gold Medal for Gaelic writing was, clearly, open to overseas entrants.

explains why Calum's writing was posted hopefully across the Atlantic Ocean. But only the application and literacy of the teenaged Calum MacLeod explain why, after the American adjudicators had deliberated over scores of entries, he was awarded first prize in the competition and the Celtic Society of New York's G. Duncan MacLeod Medal, engraved with the words 'Torran School 1925, won by Malcolm MacLeod', was mailed back to South Arnish.

On the Sabbath he and his family worshipped at the Free Presbyterian Mission Hall in Torran, where the lay preacher conducted services entirely in Gaelic except during the Glasgow Fair holiday in July, when relatives from the urban south would be visiting and a few words of English might be inserted to make them feel welcome.

Calum MacLeod was a curious, intelligent, imaginative and articulate child. He devoured knowledge hungrily. He learned, as empirically as any energetic child in an open countryside, all that there was to learn about the natural history of his environment. He learned, chiefly by word of mouth, chiefly in Gaelic, the recent and ancient histories of his people, and he never forgot a word. His cinema, theatre and television were the legends told by older people at night, in their house or in his. 'That was how time was spent in the winter time,' a neighbour and contemporary recalled. 'People going visiting. We used to call it "tighinn a cheilidh a nochd a dh' Arnais" ("coming to visit tonight in Arnish"). When we were young we looked on

the ceilidh as just going visiting and talking and telling
stories. Today you look on a ceilidh as singing and
playing and drinking and whatever you like. But in
those days it was a "visiting" that we called it.'

'When I was young', Calum MacLeod would tell the
BBC radio presenter Alan Hamilton in 1980, 'all the
young boys gathered to a ceilidh in a crofter's house.
And there would be a competition amongst the boys as
to who could make this knot or that knot, or who
could mend a herring net. And next night perhaps we
would go into another house where there would be an
old soldier who was in the First World War, and he
would entertain us telling how he bayoneted the Ger-
mans, being left-handed, and whatnot. There was a
storyteller in each village, if not more.'

There were occasional dramas in this bucolic childhood. Bulls were the biggest and, human beings ex-
cepted, the most valuable domesticated animals to
enter a crofting township. They were a fearsome,
unforgettable feature of any such rural upbringing.
Bulls evinced a visceral physical power. Bulls were
testosterone on the hoof. The presence of bulls was
inevitably immortalised in oral legend.

'One evening,' Calum would recall, 'two girls went
to look for their cows, and reported that there was a
tin stuck on the bull's nose.

'The bull found it on the beach and seemingly was
licking it on the inside, and two or three of his teeth
penetrated it. Well, I didn't know what to do. When
anybody touched it the animal gave a terrific roar and

cleared everybody away and out of it. But finally my father went home and he got a coil of rope, 120 fathom. And he says, "Put a bowline on this rope and round the animal's neck and then direct it into the potato land, soft land." And he tied the other end to a big rowan tree.

'So this was done. The bull ran out of the sand with the noose round its neck and careered into the arable land. So every crofter was on top of him, taking off the tin! But while it lived that animal would not care to see anybody going near its head again. And throughout the night I woke up several times imagining a raging bull charging me in bed!'

There is no need to mythologise or search for metaphors in the fact that bulls and the dreams and stories attached to bulls would pursue Calum Mac-Leod up to and including the very week of his death. That was the nature of bulls. Bulls in Arnish and Torran backed over cliffs rather than be dusted with delousing powder – and climbed back again un-scathed. One white bull lost its balance, rolled down a hillside and came to rest against a stone wall with its legs in the air. The crofters rushed to demolish the wall; the bull rolled over once again, got to its feet and walked away with no greater damage than a twisted horn. Bulls seemed indestructible. Seventy years after his boyhood, Calum MacLeod's friends and relatives would be taught in the most Hebridean of fashions that bulls were not.

The dutiful, attentive young Calum MacLeod also

watched his father pursue the family craft of stone-masonry. 'In my younger days I was often working with my father, you see, building stone dykes and outside buildings and the like of that, and I took some note of what was being done – how they were joined together and how they were put together and the like of that.' Both his father, Donald, and his grandfather, Malcolm, worked with two other men to create finely crafted stonework, such as the striking wall that they built in the late 1890s around the Free Presbyterian Manse at Holoman in central Raasay, which would stand proud into the twenty-first century. The young Calum MacLeod would come to understand that this skill, and its usefulness to the estate, was largely responsible for his family's continuing presence in the island being tolerated by successive notoriously intolerant factors. 'Our family were left on Raasay in the olden times because they were dry-stone dykers,' he would say in 1973. 'And maybe that's in their blood going back a long, long way, as the saying goes.'

The Book of Hours

Submitted Petition dated 3rd June by residenters of
Raasay appealing for the construction of a Road from
Brochel Castle to the Island of Fladda – a distance of
3½ miles or thereby . . .

Minutes of Roads Committee of
Inverness County Council, 1 July 1931

The first fifth of a mile of the old footway from Brochel
Castle to Arnish wound northwards up a short but
steep and densely wooded incline. In the 1960s it
presented Calum MacLeod with possibly his sternest
challenge. The pathway immediately beyond the end
of the adopted council road, an existing thoroughfare
for which the council had accepted responsibility for
improvement and maintenance, was little more than a
sheep-track through trees. The initial, essential act of
widening it by ten feet did not just involve clearing
shrubbery and levelling land: it required the excavation and removal – all by pick and shovel and hand –

of the deep and stubborn root systems of elderly birch. And then the resultant pits had to be filled in with boulders and surface stones.

It was literally an uphill task of clearance and reclamation, and it took Calum more than half a year. On 15 April 1966 Colonel Basil Reckitt, who had recently bought as a holiday home the old manse at Holoman in central Raasay, entered in his diary, 'The first quarter-mile of the path from Brochel has been made up to a base for a surface to take cars. Calum MacLeod has been working on it for the last six months, and has done a remarkable job in that time. At the present rate of progress he will finish the rough road as far as Arnish in about five years.'

Colonel Reckitt's well-intentioned forecast would prove overly optimistic. Once Calum reached the top of the slope he looked onto a further half-mile of exposed terrain which, before it disappeared over the near horizon into a challenging glen, while comparatively defoliated, was comprised instead of trembling peat bog irregularly punctuated by large outcrops of granite. There would be no straight and comfortable course over biddable earth between Brochel and Arnish.

Below this natural belvedere, this hilltop that marked the completion of his first fifth of a mile of foundation, the sea stretched eastwards towards the Scottish mainland. Calum MacLeod was a native historian. He had seen and heard of momentous traffic on those waters just forty-five years before.

*   *   *

One March morning in 1921 a small boat set sail from Acarsaid Thioram on the west coast of Rona. The skiff went more or less due south, into the Inner Sound of Raasay, with Applecross in the distance on its port bow and the empty shielings and cleared townships of North and South Screapadal lowering above its starboard gunwales.

The men aboard continued southerly down this ghostly coastline, past the broken stone remains of the homes at Hallaig and Leac, until they reached the accessible shore at Eyre. There they beached the boat. They went ashore, and on the old sites at Fearns, which seventy years previously had been the most populous part of Raasay, they erected temporary dwellings. Making plans for more permanent homes, they began to stake out the good, soft land. The adults among them were ex-servicemen who had returned in 1919 from the First World War. After having spent much of their lives looking hopefully back over at Raasay from the shores of Rona, they had had enough.

The Raasay Raids, as the Raasay Raiders knew full well, were not unique. All across the Hebrides, in Uist, Harris, Skye and Lewis, returned servicemen had by 1920 and 1921 run out of patience. Before the war they had been assured of new crofts; during the war the survivors among them had been promised a home fit for heroes; but after the war they came back from Flanders and the North Atlantic Ocean to the familiar, depressing status quo of domestic squalor, disease and restricted land. They had not fought and watched their neighbours die for that.

The Raasay archipelago was by 1921 owned by the Coatbridge ironmasters William Baird and Co. Raasay's considerable and diverse mineralogy – a subject which would, on various levels, come to intrigue Calum MacLeod of Arnish – had long been known to include seams of iron ore. When the last remnants of the Wood family decided to sell up in 1911, Baird & Co. bought the islands. Letting out the Big House, the Home Farm, the sheep farm and the sporting rights, they set about turning the south of Raasay into an iron mine.

The enterprise quickly failed, and would have failed even more quickly if the First World War had not brought with it both increased demand for iron and free labour in the form of German prisoners-of-war, who had been shipped into the newly built mining village of Inverarish, half of which was hastily converted into a PoW camp. At the end of the war the surviving prisoners were returned home and the price of Raasay ore plummeted from its 1916 value of six shillings a ton to four pence a ton.* The substantial mining works were given in 1920 to the 'care and maintenance' of three locally retained men. They would never be reopened.

William Baird & Co., who had never had any interest in the people of the islands of Raasay, Fladda

---

* The market price of Raasay iron ore had therefore collapsed in peacetime to roughly 5 per cent of its wartime value.

and Rona, by 1921 had no interest in any aspect of the estate whatsoever. Luckily, others did. The Scottish Land Court, which had been established in 1912 to assist in resolving disputes relating to agricultural tenancies, including matters relating to crofts, had in 1919 visited Rona, slashed the rents there and reported that it was 'entirely unsuited for a settlement of small-holders'. The Scottish Board of Agriculture, emboldened by a postwar Land Settlement Act which gave it some ability to purchase compulsorily from reluctant owners land for crofting, was in protracted negotiation with both Baird & Co. and the people of Rona about the creation of crofts in Raasay when those small boats set sail in 1921. Letters had already been posted early in 1921 from Rona to the Board of Agriculture in Edinburgh, warning that if the good land in Raasay could not be legitimately given, then it would be informally seized and squatted. In January of that year the board was warned following angry public meetings in Rona and northern Raasay, 'we will take the law into our own hands and make a general raid in both sheep and Home Farm in Raasay, which is for a number of years now let to [a] sporting English gentleman, who rears calves with the milk we should be getting to feed our little children'.

And they did. A series of exploratory, inquisitive and quite conspicuous visits by men from Rona to the old Home Farm and to the southlands at Eyre and Fearns which began as early as March 1920 – which Baird's factor, who was still resident, considered to be

a 'bluff', and which in the case of the Home Farm,
upon which they had no recent claim, it possibly was –
culminated in more permanent removals in the following year. Once the men had set up camp at Fearns they
cautiously brought down their wives and families. In
the subsequent words of their lawyer they 'took possession of the lands from which their forefathers had
been cleared, they removed [the sheep farm's] stock
very carefully and avoided any unnecessary loss. They
offered fair rent for the lands.'

Even at this time of widespread Hebridean land
skirmishes, the Raasay Raids attracted a great deal
of national and local attention and sympathy. What
happened in the months and years following the spring
of 1921 was of special interest to an intelligent schoolboy in the north of Raasay – a schoolboy who could,
throughout that summer, have watched from the coast
a few hundred yards from his family croft the skiffs
containing agricultural implements, household goods
and their owners tacking back and forth, like maritime
pantechnicons, between Rona and Eyre.

And what happened was that the raiders were
themselves raided. As their numbers grew in March
and April, William Baird & Co. and their tenant of
Raasay House and Home Farm and current sheep-
farmer, Captain Rawnsley of Lincolnshire, resorted
to the law. Interdicts were issued against five of the
men, ordering them off Baird's land in Raasay. They
were never likely to heed them. On 12 July the sheriff-
substitute at Portree in Skye found the five guilty in

absentia of breach of interdict and issued warrants for their arrest. When, six weeks later, those men had neither given themselves up nor evacuated the south end of Raasay a detachment of police landed on the island. The policemen would have been visible from Fearns for a long time before they disembarked. Upon arriving there they discovered that the raiders had 'erected several rude houses for the occupation of themselves and their children, and the numbers of the invaders [had] been considerably augmented within the last week or two'. The five indicted men, however, were nowhere to be found. They were, the officers and the press were told, 'in hiding' in 'the hills and caves of the island'.

This would have been daunting news for the authorities. Raasay is not a large island, but its topography is as wild and inscrutable as any of the Hebrides. Five men who knew that landscape, and who had the support of virtually every other inhabitant, could have remained at large indefinitely in this place without a permanent police or military presence. But they were not interested in becoming outlaws. They wished, merely, to be crofters. 'The men repudiate any suggestion', reported a correspondent to the *Scotsman*, 'as to their being regardless of law and order, but they contend that the course they have taken was the only one open to them in the circumstances . . . They express regret that the Board of Agriculture has delayed so long to enforce its powers . . . If the Board were to assure them that they would get land peaceably and legally, the men say they are willing to do everything possible to conform with the order of the Court and to show their respect for law and order. They say, however, that they could not remain any longer in Rona . . .'

Following widespread publicity and interventions,* on Monday 19 September the five Raasay fugitives gave themselves up to a second visiting detachment of police officers. They were taken to Portree amid 'some

---

* The prime minister, David Lloyd George, happened that September to be on vacation in Gairloch on the neighbouring Ross-shire mainland. This normally unremarkable fact became celebrated, not only in Raasay but internationally, owing to the troublesome and extremely public peace negotiations with President Eamon de Valera's provisional government in Ireland which Lloyd George conducted partly from his Wester Ross holiday retreat, and which led to him convening in Inverness on 7 September 1921 the only British Government Cabinet meeting ever to be held outside London.

Lloyd George, who was immersed in lengthy translations of de Valera's Gaelic-language assertions of Irish independence, suddenly received in Gairloch another long complaint from a smaller and hitherto less troublesome province of the Gaidhealtachd. The parish councillor, John M. MacLeod of Raasay, a shoemaker who lived in Clachan but had been born in Rona, took the opportunity of the prime minister's proximity to write – in English – and tell him that just twenty-five miles away men who in 1914 had 'responded willingly to the call of duty' were even now being 'hunted like vermin for asserting their right to live in the country which gave them birth, and in defence of which they fought so well'. John MacLeod received a quick acknowledgement and the assurance that David Lloyd George would give the matter his attention. An offer to send a delegation from Raasay to Gairloch, in a small but singular echo of the conference which Lloyd George was attempting to set up with the Irish, was politely declined.

pathetic scenes, their wives, children and friends following them as far as they could'. Upon their arrival in Skye 'a considerable crowd, obviously in sympathy with the arrested men, followed them all the way to the [Portree] prison gates'.

Two days later, at nine in the evening of 22 September, the five men's case was adjourned until 6 October and they were released pending trial. 'Although the hour was late,' reported the *Scotsman*'s diligent correspondent, 'a number of their friends, who had been awaiting anxiously the result of the Court, received them with cheers, and the men were carried shoulder high to the Caledonian Hotel, Portree, where they stayed overnight.' Early next morning the five were piped down to Portree harbour, where they boarded the steamer back to Raasay. It discharged them after an hour's sailing at the ironworks' pier, which had been built and then abandoned by William Baird & Co., and an hour after that they would have been back in Fearns, where 'the community now number[ed] about 40'.

The cases of Malcolm MacKay, John MacKay, Donald MacLeod, John MacSwan and Donald MacLeod were duly heard by Sheriff Valentine in Portree two weeks later. Before passing sentence the sheriff said that 'in some respects the position is difficult', but that he had no alternative but to uphold the letter of the law. Sheriff Valentine found in favour of the pursuers, William Baird and Captain Rawnsley, and sentenced each of the five men to a fine of £15, approximately £450 in real terms today. If after twenty-one days the fine was unpaid, they would have to serve forty-two days' imprisonment.

They did not, it goes without saying, have that kind of money – John MacSwan's annual rental in Rona, for instance, had been no more than £3. But, even if their supporters could have raised the £75, there was never any question of the Raasay Raiders paying it. Their cause had become a moral crusade. And so, on the afternoon of Wednesday, 9 November 1921, the five men were taken under police escort to Inverness Jail. They were met at the town's railway station 'by ex-servicemen, who loudly cheered them as they entered the conveyance to take them to prison'.

A week later the Government attempted to seek a compromised solution, suggesting to the imprisoned men's lawyer, Donald Shaw, that they relinquish their squatted holdings at Fearns in return for a promise of new land elsewhere. The five men refused. 'It is impossible', they wrote from Inverness Jail on 17 November, 'for us to give any undertaking because we have no place to go to and as you know our families are in Raasay, our cattle is there, our peats and potatoes is there and we cannot bear to see our children exposed to the four winds of Heaven.'

They were released, all five of them, on the morning of Tuesday, 20 December. They were fêted from the gates of the jail to Inverness Railway Station, where they boarded the train to Kyle of Lochalsh. They received another 'rousing reception' at Kyle that afternoon. They caught the steamer to Raasay and disembarked at around 6.00 p.m. They were met there by 'a large crowd of sympathisers, who had been patiently waiting at the pier for the arrival of the boat. They gave the men a warm welcome. In honour of the raiders, bonfires were lighted in Raasay and Skye, and threw their lurid glare all night across the stormy waters that separate the islands from the mainland.'

As a ten-year-old schoolboy in Arnish, Calum undoubtedly saw those bonfires before being packed off to bed. And Calum MacLeod certainly followed the rest of this story. The five men returned that December, not to Rona, but, naturally, to their families and friends in Fearns. They were still in breach of interdict and therefore still liable to be rearrested and reimprisoned. But the landowners and the Board of Agriculture had had enough bad publicity. Two months later, early in February 1922, William Baird & Co. offered, through their representative Donald Shaw, to rehouse the five men and their families, pending their permanent resettlement on crofting land, rent-free in the deserted company mining cottages at Inverarish. The men accepted, and on 10 February horses and carts belonging to Bairds transported their household goods from Fearns down past the empty mineworks to the village – and former PoW camp – of Inverarish.

A year later, in February 1923, Bairds sold all of Raasay, Rona and Fladda but the mineral rights and mining works to the Scottish Rural Workers Approved Society, whose trustees promptly sublet the land to the

Board of Agriculture. The selling price was £16,150 –
a purchasing power of around £600,000 in today's
money – just over half the sum that George Rainy had
spent just seventy-seven years earlier, and almost exactly a quarter of the £65,000 that Edward Wood had
paid for the islands less than fifty years before, in 1876.
Security of crofting tenure and the prospect of compulsory land resettlement had made Highland crofting
estates dubious investments.

The Board of Agriculture promptly created new
holdings at Fearns, Eyre, Suisnish, Inverarish, Brochel,
Glame and Oscaig. The island of Rona quickly emptied. The census of 1921, the year of the raids, showed
98 people living there. Ten years later there were only
16. And in 1951 the first census after the Second
World War showed Rona once again to be empty
of everybody but its lighthouse keepers.

The effect of the Raasay Raids on the family and
neighbours of Calum MacLeod was both symbolic
and practical. On the first level they represented at
least three essential lessons: that bureaucracy and
distant officialdom, however well-intentioned, were
unreliable sources of assistance; that, in contrast,
direct action worked; and that direct action – taking
matters into one's own hands, whatever the short-term
cost – was at times more than simply feasible: it could
be the only way to progress. None of these lessons
would be new to a 1920s crofting family in the north
of Raasay. But rarely had they been so vividly illustrated.

Practically, the success of the raids in transplanting people from Rona back to Raasay splintered and scattered the community in which Calum MacLeod was growing up. Nobody begrudged their neighbours' escape from poverty and disease in Rona, but from 1921, as Raasay's demographic pendulum took a giant lurch towards reviving the south and isolating the north, Calum's homelands were a quieter and a lonelier place. Arnish, Torran, Fladda and Kyle Rona steadily returned to their pre-clearance populations of the 1820s and 1830s. Those had been and still were sustainable levels of inhabitance. Each township could allow only a small handful of families to edge above the poverty level by farming the available land and sea. But since the 1850s and 1860s – within many surviving lifetimes – the north of Raasay, Fladda and Rona had been, insofar as its native people were concerned, the whole of Raasay. Now, in the 1920s, with the evacuation of Rona the trend swung back in favour of the south. And that pendulum, as few people had reason to guess at the time, would continue to creep in one direction only. It never swung back.

But as he noticed the sudden social vacuum immediately to his north, the young Calum MacLeod would not have had much time or self-pity spare to regret it. There was a life to lead at Arnish, a schooling to get and a living to earn.

Even without the hundred or more people in Rona, this small region was and would remain for several decades a busy and a viable community. Calum's grandfather Malcolm and grandmother Kate moved south to a former estate house at Clachan in 1927 – 'they just got a house, they were too old to do croft work' – but Kate's brother John's family moved into their Arnish cottage, and Calum's father, Donald, came back from sea in 1930 to work as a crofter-fisherman. More than a hundred people still lived in northern Raasay, Fladda and (occasionally) Eilean Tighe.

Beyond the woodlands, arable plots and green pasture of Arnish, Torran and Fladda it was a bare and unpromising few square miles of earth. Round hills rolled from coast to coast, covered with heather and black peat bog and broken by blisters of bedrock. The small hills were dotted with lochans and serrated by shallow crevasses, apparently offering little to the settled pastoralist. But to the handful of families who remained there, it was almost enough. Those hills offered rough grazings for cattle and for sheep, and their peat bogs gave fuel. Small plots of sheltered land could be reclaimed, fertilised and cut into corrugated channels deep enough for a few vegetables to take root. And around them, all around them, there was always the sea, with its lobsters and its shoals of fish, its broad inviting avenues to distant wage-paying fisheries, to the merchant navy and to the manufactories of the south and east.

The community had learned not only how to survive in this place, but also how to live relatively full and healthy lives. John Cumming was born in 1915 at

Doire Dubh, 'a rather gloomy hamlet on the east side of Kyle Rona'. Even there, on the farthest outcrop of inhabited Raasay, the Cummings had neighbours for a short time during John Cumming's boyhood – 'a family of Gillieses'. The father of that Gillies family, who had been christened Alastair but was nicknamed 'Suilag', 'was building a new house, a very imposing building, but like the Tower of Babel it was never finished, as the family moved to the south of the island'.

Alastair Gillies's wife, Peggy, John Cumming recalled in 1996, was a healer. 'Peggy Benton was from Skye; she had a good knowledge of herbal healing. I'm sure she was a descendant of the Bethuens or Beatons, the famous physicians to the Lords of the Isles.* Peggy

---

* During the fourteenth- and fifteenth-century patriarchy of the Lordship of the Isles, and in the clan system which survived it, many professions were hereditary. Medicine was one of them. This discipline was the province of the MacBeth, MacBeatha, Beaton or Bethune family. Their role pre-dated the Lordship of the Isles: one Patrick MacBeth/Beaton had been the court doctor of King Robert Bruce in the 1310s. After the lordship's demise the family continued to ply its inherited trade in Islay and Mull – where they settled for the surname MacBeth – and in Skye, where they finally became Beatons. It has been widely assumed that the last of them to practise the family skills in their communities was Neil Beaton of Skye, who died in 1763 and was described by Martin Martin thirty years later as an 'illiterate empiric . . . who of late is so well known in the isles and continent, for his great success in curing several dangerous distempers, though he never appeared in the quality of a physician until he arrived at the age of forty years, and then also without the advantage of education. He pretends to judge of the various qualities of plants and roots by their different tastes; he has likewise a nice   *cont'd over/*

was also an unofficial midwife, and was called out a few times during an emergency, or sometimes owing to the late arrival of the District Nurse. There were no cars in those days [nor, John Cumming might have added, any road to drive them along] and the Nurse had to walk from Glame, which was a long way from Kyle Rona. There was one occasion when they had to go for Peggy during a heavy fall of snow, and the man of the house had to carry Peggy on his back through the snow for about a mile, but she saved the baby. That baby is now a woman over seventy years of age and living still on the island.'

Within this microcosmic culture the small but separate villages retained their own identities in idiosyn-

cont'd observation of the colours of their flowers, from which he learns their astringent and loosening qualities; he extracts the juice of plants and roots after a chemical way, peculiar to himself, and with little or no charge.'

From John Cumming's account it would seem that the Beaton family's medical aptitude did not die with Neil, but was still being practised by their clanswoman in the north of Raasay in the first half of the twentieth century. Some idea of the 'alternative' medical aid dispensed by such as Peggy Benton may be found in *I Remember*, John 'London' Nicolson's memoirs of his Torran boyhood in the 1920s and 1930s. Treacle and vinegar were favoured ingredients, cods' livers were melted down for their oil, seal oil was rubbed into wheezy chests, ringworm was dabbed with ink, chrysanthemum leaves were eaten for headaches, cobwebs stemmed bleeding. Modern treatments were not despised: castor oil was a primary treatment of any internal upset, and 'iodine was the first line of defence for injuries'. Lint, zinc ointment and Germolene were also kept to hand. Any or all of these were usually more efficacious than waiting for the district nurse to walk up from Brochel or Glame.

cratic ways. Some communities ate 'braxy mutton'*
and dried dogfish, which would be rejected by the
handful of families in their neighbouring townships.
The people of Arnish were partial to conger eel, despite
the bones and despite the fact that this delicacy was
judged unsuitable for pregnant women. Calum
MacLeod's mother, Sheila, put raisins in her mealie
puddings, which was also unacceptable in Torran,
where they preferred steamed cod's head stuffed with
cod's liver, oatmeal and onions, while spurning, as
also did many in Kyle Rona, the conger eel which was
popular elsewhere. Calum MacLeod himself retained a
lifelong fondness for 'the lovely dark meat' of cormor-
ant, or 'scart' as the species was known locally. He
would shoot the birds – with notable accuracy – from a
high rock beside Loch Arnish, after which they would
be skinned, the tail-end chopped off – otherwise it had
an overly fishy flavour – and made into 'excellent
broth' which was deemed particularly efficacious in
the treatment of the common cold.

These were antique diets, but Calum MacLeod grew
up in a world where the distance between history and
the present was often truncated; where large fragments
of the past were tangible and everyday. There was no
piped water. It was drawn daily from a number of
ancient wells. The wells were often specialised:

* Braxy is an acute ovine disease also known as bradsot. In this
instance the term 'braxy mutton' refers to the meat of a sheep
which has not been deliberately slaughtered but has died apparently of natural causes.

one would provide good-quality drinking water; another might be used only for washing. One day, said John Cumming, 'I found an old musket hidden in the heather on a ledge above the well from which we got our drinking water. I can't remember anything about what happened to that gun. How long that gun was hidden there is anybody's guess, probably from after Culloden when people were prohibited from carrying guns.' The Battle of Culloden was fought in 1746. In this place, in some ways, it was closer than the twentieth-century mainland.

There was a postal and telegram service, but no tap water. There were local government rates, but no electricity. There was a telephone wire, but no vehicular access road. When Calum MacLeod was twelve years old, in 1923, his neighbour John Nicolson was born in Torran 'in the last occupied black house in Raasay'. Just as Calum was the great-grandson of the Charles MacLeod who testified to Lord Napier's Commission in 1883, John Nicolson was a grandson of the Murdo Nicolson of Torran who had told Lord Napier that he wished 'for a better place'.

And just as life in Arnish had hardly changed between the times of Charles and Calum MacLeod, so in Torran it had remained for John as it had been for Murdo Nicolson. John Nicolson would recollect the strict, time-tried itinerary laid out by the unwritten Book of Hours of crofting life. 'The thing that I think of today', he said in 2005, 'is the way that the people worked. They had a method with everything, when I think back on it today. They didn't wait for the weather or the seasons – they did things in stages all through the year. Once New Year was passed, the fishermen were away at the creels or whatever they were doing and after exactly three months on the water, once the end of March came, all fishing stopped and they started the croft work.

'They turned the ground with the "cas-chrom" [traditional foot plough], went down to the seaweed for manure, carried it up to the crofts, started planting the potatoes in the first or second week of April. All the croft work was finished by the end of April, the seed was sown, everything.

'And as soon as that was finished, they started doing the fencing – the fencing, in those days, wasn't what we now know as a fence. If there was a wire fence, oh boy! that was something. Fencing then was stone dykes or earth dykes, one or the other, the dykes to keep the sheep out and the dykes to keep the cows out.

'So, by the first week in May, the sheep that were on the crofts were taken away to the hill and they were there for the rest of the summer. After that was done, you then started on cutting the peats about the middle of May. Fair weather or foul, the peats were cut. More often than not, when you think back on it, it was good weather in May – not brilliant every year, but quite often it was. I remember because we were barefooted then – once the first of May came, off came our boots and we were bare-foot.

'While they were cutting the peats the lambs were all

sorted out, they were castrated and all the rest of it – marked out so that everyone knew which was whose. They cut the peats and then, by the beginning of June, the drying peats were being lifted and then made into stooks out on the hill. When we were in school, once we got our summer holidays in July, that was our job, to take the peats home and put them into a shed – it wasn't a shed as we call a shed today but it was a building with a thatched roof on it and they took home as much of that peat as they possibly could so that when they started the harvest work, nobody had to go to the peats, it was already there.

'The harvest work, more often than not, started after what they called the Portree Communion which was the second Sabbath in August – the harvest work started then and it carried on until the potatoes were lifted at the beginning of October or the end of September. This was how they worked things. The sheep that were out on the hill were then taken in on the crofts, and they were on the crofts all winter. Today you see sheep on the crofts twelve months of the year, which I don't think is right – that wasn't what we were brought up to. The cattle were the same. I always remember we had two cows – I think it was two cows and a follower we were allowed.

'More often than not the potatoes were lifted if at all possible before October, because at this time they were getting ready to start the lobster fishing. Those who were at the lobsters went away in the early morning and they were back by three in the afternoon or something like that – rowing most of the time because a sail took up too much room in the boat. The boat that my father was on was working about eighty lobster creels, and it was twenty each that they had, if I remember right, there were four of them in the boat.

'New Year was a holiday, but if it was New Year at the beginning of the week, on the Sabbath, it was very seldom that they went out that day. They would go out next day and the day before. The other thing we looked forward to was seeing our cousins coming home from Glasgow in the summer. We looked forward to this because they were there for a month, so we looked forward to this when we were going to school. The same happened in other houses round about, the summer visits of the families that had left and gone away to Glasgow, Edinburgh, Aberdeen or wherever.'

John Cumming and his brothers and sisters walked four miles each morning of the academic term down the track from Kyle Rona to Torran School, which they attended with Calum MacLeod and John Nicolson, and then each weekday afternoon they walked four miles back again. In places, John Cumming would recall, the old cart path which George Herbert Wood had spent £395 on improving half a century earlier had all but disappeared: 'there was no road, only bogs and sheep tracks'.

'It was a long, long walk for them,' said John Nicolson. 'It was the same for the people from Brochel

Castle in the south, except the Brochel Castle people perhaps had a better path to walk on, to and from Torran, than the Kyle Rona crowd did.' The track did have some compensations. As John Cumming and his siblings and their neighbours from Kyle Rona lived more than three miles from school they would normally have qualified for transport provision from Inverness County Council. Local authority school transport being, in their circumstances, inconceivable – and the liberal Seumas Ruadh MacKinnon being their teacher – 'we were never on time reaching school, we took advantage of being outside the three-mile limit. We didn't get punished for being late.'

Calum MacLeod left the cheerful Gaelic anarchy of Torran School in 1926 with his Celtic Society of New York medal and subscribed at the age of fifteen to the life for which his schoolday evenings and weekends spent on the croft, the hill and the water had been an apprenticeship: the full and unrelenting seasonal vocation of the adult male crofter-fisherman. He went to work on a creel and ground-net fishing boat, firstly with the men of the Graham family of Torran on their *Isabella*, and later, in their own vessel, the *Flora*, with his father Donald and brother Ronald.

Creel boats, as we have seen, were effectively a part-time operation. The crew of three or four would set off in the winter mornings and return by mid-afternoon. Lobster creels were – and remain – underwater traps for crustaceans. They were cages with a couple of one-way entrances, baited inside with some roughly preserved fish such as mackerel, and lowered down from a buoy through the cold water to lie on the inshore seabed. The job of the lobster fisherman was to haul them up as regularly as possible, retrieve any captured lobster, rebait the creels and return them to the sea. Creels were naturally homemade and handmade, and damaged creels were restored onshore during the long winter evenings.

'Wood would come ashore [as flotsam] mostly,' recalled John Nicolson of Torran, 'or the men would be over to Portree in Skye to get a packing case to make lobster creels. The creel frames were made with wood and the netting was made with what you got on the trees – willow fibre and the rest of it. So that kept them going at night-time during the winter, those that were working with lobster creels. And if he wasn't making creels my father used to mend his herring nets during the winter, and the others were the same – that was the nets ready to go out when they started fishing for the herring.'

The *Flora*, the boat which Calum would crew with his father and brother, was a substantial 35-foot vessel brought in from the traditional fishing village of Tarbert, Loch Fyne in Argyllshire. She moored alongside the *Isabella* and the *Fladda Maid* mainly in the protected southern narrows of Fladda, and in the short months of summer calm at Port an Altainn in Loch Arnish.

When Calum MacLeod first went out into the Sound of Raasay as a stakeholder, rather than a schoolboy in a boat, lobsters were sold in Portree for roughly twelve shillings and sixpence – sixty-two and a half new pence [around £17 in the early twenty-first century] – a dozen or a shilling – five new pence – each. But although lobsters were in the 1920s comparatively plentiful, no creel – and no boat – rendered a lobster at every haul, and the lobsters from north Raasay were not always acceptable by the time they reached their distant market. 'They used to go over with the lobsters to Portree on a Monday, maybe every fortnight,' says John Nicolson. 'They weren't sold in Portree, they were sent off to Billingsgate in London and sometimes the card would come back from there with "lobsters dead" written on it, and then they got nothing for them. That didn't happen often, but it happened.'

Calum grew up in a mixed economy. His life was sustained by a combination of subsistence vegetables and grain from the family croft, game and domesticated meat, common seasonal fish such as herring and mackerel when the great shoals arrived, and a local social system of barter and exchange which took care of most surpluses. His life was enhanced by occasional forays into the world of cash. There were several sources of banknote and coin available to Calum MacLeod and his neighbours, other than shipping lobsters to Billingsgate. Sheep wool and the sheep themselves were sold at market, along with excess male cattle. The crews of the three ground-net fishing boats from northern Raasay, the *Flora*, the *Isabella* and the *Fladda Maid*, netted white fish and herring for sale in Skye or on the mainland. Three local men were employed part-time by the Royal Mail to collect the outgoing post from Kyle Rona, Fladda and Castle, deliver it to Seumas Ruadh MacKinnon at the sorting office – the middle bedroom of his raucous schoolhouse in Torran – and take the incoming mail back home again. There were also occasional council and other public-sector contracts to be had.

And there were the whelks. Like many a Hebridean teenager before and since, Calum MacLeod supplemented his income from the whelks. Whelks are winkles in the Highland vernacular: small edible gastropods which eat seaweed and therefore flourish in the kelp forests on the shoreline of north-western Scotland. They are prized, both for their meat and as a garnish, by seafood restaurants. When Calum MacLeod collected them by hand at low tide off the shore of northern Raasay during the months of deepest winter – the whelk season is short and chilly – in the mid 1920s, the wholesalers paid him seven shillings and sixpence (equivalent to around £14 today) for two bushels of whelks. A bushel is a unit of volume equivalent in this case to eight imperial gallons. Each tiny living whelk – for empty shells had, of course, to be rejected – was plucked by hand from the thickets of weed in the January sea. Calum's sacks or creels of whelks were then left, hopefully preserved, in the cold and the wet just below the high-tide mark until the time came to ship them by the double-bushel to market and collect his seven-and-six per brace.

In 1927, when he was sixteen years old, Calum MacLeod had his first stab at one of the salaried and pensionable public-service posts which were so prized by men and women who were otherwise wholly dependent on the harvests of a thin soil and a fertile but unwelcoming sea. The *Isabella*, upon which he crewed, became the Rona Lighthouse Attending Boat.

There had been a lighthouse on the northern tip of Rona since 1857. Its keepers were by 1927 the only inhabitants of Rona who were destined to remain there. They were served by one of the local fishing boats, which, as the Rona Lighthouse Attending Boat, was paid a retainer to take the keepers to and from Portree every two months at the start and finish of their shifts, and to keep them supplied with provisions. This job had always previously been done by one of the Rona boats, but the rapid depopulation of Rona in the 1920s led to it being offered to the Grahams of Torran. 'They got paid extra for that,' says John Nicolson. 'What it was I can't remember – it would be peanuts really, but they did this once a month so there was something coming in.'*

This combination of subsistence farming and hired labour was sustainable only for so long as northern Raasay and Fladda maintained a certain level of

---

* Ronald MacLennan of Rona had told the Deer Park Commission thirty years earlier that he received five shillings a week as an 'attendant boatman' on the 'lighthouse packet'.

population. Postmen would not be employed if there was nobody to send or receive mail. Schoolteachers would have no jobs if there were no schoolchildren. Boats could not take to the water without crews. The social system of barter and exchange would collapse if there was nobody to barter and exchange with. Much of the fabric of crofting activity, from gathering sheep to peat cutting and harvesting, was communal and dependent upon a healthy diversity of age groups. 'The townships of Brochel, South Arnish, North Arnish, Torran and Kyle Rona', wrote John 'London' Nicolson of Torran in the late 1980s, 'combined their labour resources like a workers' cooperative, for potato-planting, seed-sowing and raking in the spring . . . there was a repeat performance in the autumn with potato-lifting. A neighbourly helping hand was given with haystacks or cornstacks to an older or less fortunate crofter.'

It began to dawn on the inhabitants of northern Raasay and Fladda that since the Board of Agriculture had taken over the bulk of the Raasay Estate nobody was paying much attention to the surviving small communities north of Brochel Castle. Central and southern Raasay were being repopulated apace. Families were returning to the green lands of their grandparents. But, to the north of George Rainy's wall, the few thousand acres around Arnish and Torran and Kyle Rona, which the authorities had recently either designated or accepted as the fitting last refuge and rural ghetto of all of the native inhabitants of the archipelago, were now, apparently, of little interest. In the space of a couple of decades northern Raasay and its remnant population had become invisible. The road, and everything else, stopped at Castle.

It was a strange, inverted kind of injustice. Everybody had resented the forced overpopulation of the district. But nobody had suggested that, outside Rona itself, the answer to overpopulation was depopulation. Everybody was pleased that the Raasay Raiders had succeeded in reopening the bulk of the island. Nobody had imagined that this revolution would result in the disenfranchisement of the families they left behind. Barren, stony Rona had historically been a special case. The solution which was applicable to its hungry population was quite unsuitable to the meadows of Fladda. Those families which had been in Arnish and Torran before the MacLeod and Rainy clearances, and many of those who had not, wanted little more in the remainder of the twentieth century than the freedom to live their lives and work their land, assisted by the modest public facilities which were due to them as tax- and rate-payers. They had never asked to be expunged from the map.

On 1 July 1931, when Calum MacLeod was in his twentieth year, the roads committee of the County Council of the County of Inverness met in the Highland capital. Its distinguished members had before them a petition dated 3 June 1931. The petition was 'by residenters in Raasay appealing for the construction of a Road from Brochel Castle to the Island of

Fladda – a distance of 3½ miles or thereby'. The roads committee meeting minutes noted that this matter had been tossed back westwards to Skye District Council for their 'observations'.

Inverness County Council's roads committee was, in the 1920s and 1930s, a busy and important set of men. The arrival of the motorcar in the Highlands and – to a considerably lesser extent – the Islands of Scotland had presented the local government of this vast and often intractable land mass with a seemingly infinite series of challenges. The Highlands had been historically famous for their inaccessibility. The men who had built the first proper marching roads and paved bridle paths in the area, men such as the eighteenth-century General George Wade, Member of Parliament and extraordinary military engineer, were famous for it. Their 200-year-old highways were frequently still in use and still bore their name – a 'Wade road' remains a familiar trademark in the twenty-first century Highlands. But General Wade and his successors had not catered for motorised transport. That became the task of Inverness County Council after 1894, when the Local Government Act of that year transferred responsibility for the maintenance of public highways from the Inverness County Road Trust to the rural district authority.

Inverness County Council was only five years old in 1894. A previous Local Government Act in 1889 had established it to govern over not only mainland Inverness-shire but also the urban burghs of Fort

William, Inverness and Kingussie and the inhabited island groups of Barra, Canna, Eigg, Harris (but not Lewis, which was delivered to Ross-shire), Muck, North Uist, Raasay, Rum, St Kilda, Skye and South Uist. It would retain the same character and constituency – an immense Gaidhealtachd jurisdiction dominated by members of the mainland acreocracy and island ministers and priests – for fully eighty-six years, until a further Local Government Act swept Inverness County Council away in 1975.

In 1894 there had been very few motorcars in Britain, and those that existed could be taken out on the public highways only if preceded by a man carrying a red flag. Of course, there had been a substantial increase over the previous hundred years in the numbers of long-distance horse-drawn wheeled vehicles. But Wade's 16- to 18-foot-wide crushed stone and gravel surfaces on a convex pitched foundation could, with a minimum of maintenance, accommodate carriages, horses and carts.

The Red Flag Act was removed in 1896. Ten years later there were 16,000 motorcars in Britain. By 1920 there were just under a million. By the 1930s there were 2 million and rising. They were increasingly to be found jerking and spluttering past Loch Lomond, through the Trossachs and the Grampians and into the great uncharted motoring country of the Highlands of Scotland. And there, it was quickly discovered by motorist and county councillor alike, what had been good enough for General Wade and two centuries of his inheritors was by no means suitable for the internal combustion engine and rubber pneumatic tyres.

Highland roads had, therefore, to be rebuilt. If there was one subject upon which some of Inverness County Council's more eminent hereditary members were qualified to pronounce, it was the function and future of the motorcar. Men such as Lord Lovat and Cameron of Lochiel were among the first in the region to have experience of, as well as a personal interest in, the adventure of motoring. Perhaps partly as a result of this, main roads were rebuilt throughout the Highlands. The Islands were slower to benefit, for which the council was hardly to blame. Places like Barra, Canna and the Uists were a long sea journey away from any garage, and had few if any motorised vehicles until the 1940s. Skye, being closer to the mainland, saw them earlier. Raasay had two cars before the Second World War: one belonging to John M. MacLeod, the parish councillor and shoemaker, and one to Ewen MacRae, the piermaster at East Suisnish.

In order to cater for those gentlemen, and for the hundreds and thousands of motorists to come, Lovat, Cameron and their county council colleagues adopted, maintained and improved the existing eight miles of spinal road on Raasay between the East Suisnish pier and Brochel Castle. It is perhaps inevitable that they did not extend their responsibility north of Brochel. Inverness County Council, like its predecessor, the Inverness County Road Trust, was obliged to operate

almost entirely across a jigsaw of large private estates.
When they adopted roads they did so wherever possible upon the advice and with the cooperation of the
landowners – several of whom sat on the county
council themselves. They had, therefore, a marked
tendency to adopt and improve the roads preferred
by the estates' proprietors. In the view of all previous
private proprietors of the Raasay Estate, from the
Wood family to William Baird & Co., there was no
requirement whatsoever for a road north of Brochel
Castle. They had never attempted to provide one, and
so Inverness County Council followed suit. The public
road, like the private one, ended at Castle. At that
point the people of Torran, Fladda, Kyle Rona and
Arnish got down and walked.

At first they had asked merely to have their path-
ways north from Castle improved. In the summer of
1930 the Department of Agriculture, as the new
landlord of seven years' standing, wrote on their
behalf to Inverness County Council 'regarding the
repair of footpaths leading from Brochel to Fladda
and Kyle Rona'. The council's roads committee was
fully aware that agreeing to undertake those repairs
would be a large step towards formally adopting –
and therefore accepting permanent responsibility for
– the problematic or non-existent routes north of
Brochel Castle. So they shook their heads and threw
the matter at Skye District Council. Skye District
Council threw it back again. At a certain point in
this rally the correspondence hit the net between

them and fell limply to the ground, from there to roll
out of sight.

A year later, when, in July 1931, they received that
petition from ninety adults of north Raasay and
Fladda asking for a full public highway between
Brochel Castle and Fladda, the county council was
no more likely to agree. In September 1931 its roads
committee was presented with 're-submitted letters of
complaint regarding the condition of Raasay Roads
and petition for a new Road from Brochel Castle to
Fladda, Raasay, which were considered at the last
Meeting of the Roads Committee but regarding which
a decision was delayed pending receipt of the recom-
mendations of Skye District Council.

'Submitted letter from Skye District Council intimat-
ing that the Council are going into the question of
these Roads and in the meantime are pressing the
Department of Agriculture to make the new Road
for the benefit of their own tenants.'

Skye District Council considered that it had neither
the resources nor the remit to start building roads in
the north of Raasay. The Department of Agriculture,
in its recently acquired role as a Highland landowner,
was anxious to shuck off as many of its own established roads as possible, dropping them onto the
shoulders of the local county authorities. The department had, in fact, only just succeeded in doing exactly
that with the 2,000-yard stretch of track in the south of
Raasay between Suisnish pier and the village of
Inverarish, which Inverness County Council had

agreed that same September to 'take over . . . and add it to the List of Highways when it has been put into a proper state of repair'.

Inverness County Council considered itself in the early 1930s to be bombarded with requests for new or upgraded roads from every corner of its 4,500 square miles of challenging terrain.* The people of northern Raasay clearly believed themselves to be in receipt of a raw deal. But so did the people of Wester Ross and Skye. And there were cars in Wester Ross and Skye. There were none in northern Raasay. Its people had walked throughout the preceding centuries; what was left of them could surely walk for a few decades more.

The next small rebellion came from Fladda. The five families living there in the late 1920s had an extra grievance. Not only was there no road from the island to Brochel Castle, there was still no bridge over the short tidal narrows between Fladda and Raasay. Children from Fladda attending Torran School had perforce to run a race against the incoming sea on their way to and from school. Sometimes they missed school in the morning, and sometimes they failed to get home in the afternoon. Early in 1932, shortly after the rejection of their petition requesting a road from

---

* The square mileage of the shire of Inverness, without its offshore islands, was 4,351. It had a 1920s and 1930s population of 80,000. Inverness County Council was therefore administering a mountainous region that was over a third of the size of the countries of Holland and Belgium and four times the size of Luxembourg, but with a scattered population which was a small fraction of the European average.

Brochel, which could have brought a short bridge in its wake, the people of Fladda had asked the education committee of Inverness County Council to build them a school on the small island. The education committee noted their request, and moved on to other matters. The Fladda parents addressed the impasse by the simple expedient of keeping their children off school altogether.* If they thought that would prick either the roads or education committee into prompt action, they were wrong.

In October 1934 the staffing and organisation subcommittee of the county council recommended to the roads committee that it 'should consider the question of construction and maintenance of a proposed bridge for the use of children between the Islands of Fladda and Raasay – subject to the Department of Agriculture for Scotland being prepared to contribute 75 per cent towards construction – the remaining 25 per cent being met by the Education Committee'. The roads committee agreed that as 'the Department of Agriculture had not so far indicated their willingness to meet a proportion of

* 'There were barely twenty children at Torran School when I went there [between 1928 and 1937],' says John Nicolson. 'But there was nobody there from Fladda. They were at that time, perhaps, fighting for a school of their own, because there were children in Fladda who were coming up to school age – one boy was seven before he went to school because they refused to send him to school unless they got a teacher there in Fladda.' In the meantime, according to John 'London' Nicolson, a Fladda woman 'acted as a voluntary and unpaid teacher', giving the children fluency and literacy in both English and Gaelic.

the cost' they as councillors could 'take no action in the matter meantime'.

Some of the householders in Fladda then went on rate strike. Perhaps for this reason, perhaps because the education department was seriously concerned about the handful of children who were receiving no education, late in 1935 the council's director of education visited Fladda. Following his excursion the education committee agreed to build and staff a single-teacher school on the island. In March 1936 the Department of Agriculture allocated a piece of land for that purpose. There were by then five families in Fladda, with a total of six children between the ages of five and ten years, none of whom had ever attended school. The school was built and a teacher employed.

It would have been not much more expensive, and would certainly have satisfied more people, if instead a single-track highway and a connecting bridge or cause-way had been constructed between Fladda, Torran, Arnish and Brochel Castle. But that was not the job of the education department. It was the responsibility of the roads committee. In the mid 1930s the roads committee, in collaboration with the Department of Agriculture, relented to the extent of funding a brief, cheap track-improvement scheme between Brochel and Arnish, employing some workless Raasay men. No tractors or other mechanical aids were provided. 'It was sheer hard labour', wrote John 'London' Nicolson, 'with pick-axe, sledge-hammer, shovel, spade and barrow . . . the pay was poor and bore no relationship to the work that was done. The track had been widened slightly in parts but it was still not suitable, even as a cart road.'

The message from the roads committee of Inverness County Council in the 1930s was unmistakable. It read that while the age of motorised transport was rapidly dawning, even over Raasay, it would never shine on the north of the island. The residents of Arnish, Torran, Kyle Rona and Fladda must walk to meet the twentieth century at Brochel Castle. Their visitors, district nurses, doctors and postmen must walk from Brochel Castle into the unchanging past.

Either that, or they could move south. So they began to move south. Alasdair 'Suilag' Gillies and his wife, the healer Peggy Benton, left their new house unfinished in Kyle Rona and relocated to south Raasay, within reach of the ferry, the district nurse and the road. 'The people were gradually leaving Kyle Rona,' recalled their young neighbour John Cumming, 'some going to the south and one or two families moving to Brochel Castle. In the end only Tormod Dubh [Black Norman], known locally as Thorny, and his sister, and our own family were left. When Thorny's sister died he went away to the south end. In 1942 I went into the army. My parents by this time were getting old. My father got a croft at East Suisnish [in the south]. When father died we moved to Inverarish.'

By 1937 the roll at Torran School, which ten years earlier had numbered twenty children, had reduced to seven scholars. Umachan was emptied. One whole family of Nicolsons, including the man who would later be known as John 'London', left Torran for Oscaig in the south in 1939. 'When they left', said their cousin John Nicolson, who was sixteen at the time, 'that was a big blow to us because we had no-one of our own age to play with in the evenings, or anything like that. That was a big, big blow . . .

'But you could see that there was, not exactly unrest, but you could see people gradually drifting away, losing heart and, not only losing heart, but losing a sense of the future, because there was no work.

'There was perhaps a future in the north end of Raasay if there was a road – this three miles from Brochel Castle to Arnish or Torran, or Fladda. But there wasn't, so the population gradually haemorrhaged. My own uncle was the first, and then a family went from Arnish – two ladies who were staying on their own there went down to Inverarish. And the Kyle Rona crowd went, which was the favourite place for us to go and stay a night. And then another family went from Arnish, and the Graham family went from Torran and we were left on our own there. That was the beginning of the end really. Then it got worse after the war.'

A Few in the North
Would Not Be Catered For

After the Second World War, people came back. We all
came home, most of us came home after the war. And I
reckon myself that, if there had been a road or a road
was in the offing when the boys came home, things
could have been a lot better in the north end of Raasay.

John Nicolson, Torran

The second fifth of a mile of track between Brochel
Castle and Arnish undulated, wound and dipped over
and between stony hillocks. 'Now, if Calum was doing
anything,' a neighbour would say, 'he didn't do it the
hard way. If there was an easy way, he did it the easy
way. He was a terrific engineer. He looked at the
contours of the land, and the surface of the ground,
and if they meant going down a certain way, and it was
easier than cutting up another way, that's the way
Calum would go. The hard way may have looked
shorter, but it might still have been harder to do – so he
would dig a wee turn.'

At the end of that fifth of a mile on this exposed plateau Calum MacLeod, in the middle of the 1960s, came across a short but extremely steep slope. He overcame this challenge not by cutting straight up and over it, as a deer, a horse or a footpath might have done, but by carving a single hairpin bend out of the hillside, thereby steering his road up two relatively gentle gradients.

The inner elbow of this hairpin bend required fortifying against the slope. So Calum MacLeod then embarked upon his first substantial piece of masonry on the Brochel to Arnish road. About a hundred blocks of granite, ranging in size from a scooter wheel to the tyre of a lorry, were cut, shaped and carried or otherwise manoeuvred by hand to the roadside. Calum then built them into a solid dry-stone holding wall. The foundations of the bend in the road were laid invisibly behind this facing, and its level surface was laid on top. There can be no doubt that Calum MacLeod was unaware of the fact, but when he placed the last rock in what he would have been proud to acknowledge as an effective and well-made form of dry-stone dyke, he also laid the cornerstone of what others in future would choose to describe as a phenomenon of 'landscape art'.

It was an instantly unfamiliar sight on an extremely familiar track. The men of northern Raasay may not have had much to do with the south. But over the centuries they had walked across this plateau on their way to market, to emigration, and to war.

*   *   *

In 1939 and 1940 the Raasay men went off to war again. In the islands of the north-west of Scotland 3 September 1939 'was a very wintry day with hail and sleety showers and terrible thunder and lightning, which all seemed very fitting for a day when war was declared'. And as international hostilities commenced, domestic hostilities were suspended. There would be no more petitions or rate strikes or angry letters to the council until Hitler had been defeated.

When the Second World War broke out the 27-year-old Calum MacLeod was excused conscription as an active crofting tenant, in the reserved occupation of agricultural production. Many of his friends, neighbours and relatives from northern Raasay went to fight or to serve in the merchant navy. His brother Ronald joined the Royal Navy. John Cumming of Kyle Rona joined the army. The younger Nicolsons of Torran entered the infantry by way of the Territorial Army. 'By 1941 my brother Willie was in the Faroes, and later in England preparing for the D-Day invasions,' said John Nicolson. 'My other brother Murdo was a prisoner-of-war. Of course, I was the next to be called up. Our brother Alec was older than me, but Alec couldn't go because he was assigned [like Calum MacLeod] to look after the croft. So, like everybody else of my age at the time, I was wanting to go. That was the thought – let's get out there and help the rest, and get it over and done with. It wasn't just me, it was everybody of my age.'

They all came home. As the memorial at Suisnish in

the south of the island reminds posterity, twenty-three Raasay men had fallen in the First World War, including two from Rona, two from Kyle Rona, two from Fladda and two from Arnish. Calum MacLeod himself had lost two of his uncles in the 'Kaiser's War'. Seven Raasay men gave their lives in the Second World War, all of whom were residents at the time of the centre or the south of Raasay. The island group had made its usual disproportionately large sacrifice, but for once the north was spared.*

In 1942 a new teacher arrived at Torran School. Her name was Alexandrina Macdonald. She replaced a schoolmistress from the western mainland who had been in Torran for six years, and whose name also had been Alexandrina Macdonald. Such a confluence would have been quite implausible anywhere but in the Highlands and Islands of Scotland, where both Macdonalds and Alexandrinas abounded. In Raasay it barely merited comment. The first Alexandrina Macdonald remained in the island, settling in the village of Inverarish.

The Alexandrina Macdonald of our story, Alexandrina the second, had been born, one of a pair of twins, thirty-one years earlier in northern Skye. She was

* The disproportion of the sacrifice is best illustrated by the fact that those twenty-three servicemen sacrificed between 1914 and 1918 represented 5 per cent of the total population of the Raasay archipelago. From the whole British population of 45 million, slightly more than 700,000 men were slain. That represented a fatal casualty percentage of 1.5 per cent. It was a hideous statistic, but it was only a quarter of the toll extracted from Raasay, Fladda and Rona.

brought up in a crofthouse built by her father and uncle at Uiginish, a small and isolated village separated from the north Skye township of Dunvegan – and the mediaeval battlements of Dunvegan Castle – by an intrusive, narrow sea loch. Ina Macdonald, as she was known in Skye, was an exceptional woman. She left Dunvegan School at the age of fourteen but, unusually for a girl in 1925, then progressed by scholarship to the small but growing Portree High School, which had twenty years earlier been recognised as a Higher Grade provider of secondary education. Like Calum Mac-Leod, Ina Macdonald had as a scholar also won a Gaelic writing competition. Ina became the high school dux before passing her highers and entering a teaching course at Jordanhill Training College in Glasgow. She emerged from there with a Primary Certificate and taught in Glasgow, Glen Nevis and in the Outer Hebrides before returning to the Skye archipelago.

Back in her native islands she first of all taught the children of the three dozen people on the tiny island of Soay off the south coast of Skye. Ina Macdonald then moved to Penifiler, on the east bank of Portree Bay. A short walk from Penifiler would have put her within easy sight of the sun-dappled slopes of Raasay, to which she moved in time to begin the new school year in autumn 1942, and where, in accordance with local nomenclative custom, Alexandrina Macdonald would forever more be known not as Ina but as Lexie. 'All of the Skye people called her Ina,' her daughter, Julia, would say. 'She was Ina to her mother. To all her nieces and nephews she was Aunt Ina. And then on Raasay she was Lexie. Lexie's her Raasay name; Ina's her Skye name.'

Lexie Macdonald stayed with Torran School until Torran School was finally closed for good twenty-five years later. Her job description was formidable. John 'London' Nicolson had left Torran and moved to Oscaig in the south shortly before Lexie Macdonald's arrival. He would write that 'The one and only teacher in many Highland schools, of which Torran was but one, had to be capable of dealing with school subjects covering an age-group of five to fourteen years. The range included: Bible study, spelling, transcription, dictation, composition, recitation, history, geography, grammar, English literature and language including roots, arithmetic including mental exercises, algebra, geometry, Gaelic, reading, writing, art, nature study in and out of doors, physical exercises, gardening, singing, handcrafts, cooking.'

The requirements of state school education, even in the north of Raasay, had changed radically since the days of Seumas Ruadh MacKinnon. The 31-year-old woman who moved into Torran Schoolhouse in 1942 was extraordinarily capable, qualified and intelligent. Lexie Macdonald from Uiginish also saw no reason why living and working in such a peripheral place should compromise her personal standards. 'She was . . . different,' her daughter would say. 'She had fish knives and forks, pale green soft leather slippers and a dark green leather coat, big fur gloves and fox-fur. She would go to church and her hat always had a front leaf or feather or something sticking out of it – most of the people wore flat hats that hugged their heads. And mother always had her court shoes. She might have her wellies on for part of the way, but when she went into church, it was her court shoes. Everybody else wore flatties. So she was different. She certainly wasn't used to the labour of Arnish. I think she anticipated the job at Torran as a temporary appointment.'

Calum MacLeod of Arnish was just seven months younger than the new schoolmistress at Torran, and, like her, was single. Her anticipation of an abbreviated stay in northern Raasay was short-lived. In the words of his daughter, Calum MacLeod was 'stubborn – he was broad-minded in some ways, but at other times he had tunnel vision. If he wanted something, he went for it until he got it.'

Calum got his woman. He married the new Torran schoolmistress in April 1944. The wedding was conducted by the Reverend Donald Campbell at Torran Mission Hall, and the reception was held in Torran schoolroom. 'No broad bands of gold were allowed,' Lexie MacLeod would later write to her grandson of her wartime marriage. 'The rings were merely very slim bands of gold. Then wedding cakes, or bridescakes, posed a problem as the various ingredients were rationed. Bakers were unable to help. However, the bride's friends and also the groom's friends helped as much as possible by giving up some of their own rations. These were given to the baker who was only too glad to bake a beautiful bridescake, and put it at first on display in his shop window for a few days.'

The newly-weds moved at first into Lexie's schoolhouse at Torran. While Lexie was teaching every subject in the encyclopaedia, in English and in Gaelic, to a handful of juniors and young teenagers, Calum was growing tobacco in the schoolhouse garden. This was a remarkable, if entirely characteristic, achievement. It was remarkable because the plant genus *Nicotiana tabacum* is neither native nor suited to the British Isles. The only commercial tobacco plantations to succeed in Europe have been on the hot and humid shores of the Mediterranean. It was characteristic of the MacLeods to grow Hebridean tobacco because they believed increasingly, with every passing year, that the north of Raasay could, with God's blessing on the will and work of humanity, provide for every mortal need.

'He was once taking seaweed for manure', said John Nicolson, 'from the east side shore opposite his own house, down to the croft below his house. I said to him, one time we were over there, "Here, Calum, you have some haul there." He said, "Oh, it was fine once you got to the top at the other side, it was all downhill then!" There was no word of what it was like to go up to the top of the cliff, and that was with seaweed in a creel.

'I said, "How many creels did you take?" He said, "Oh, I'm sure I must have taken fifty or sixty creels –

about four in a day, a bhalaich, it didn't take long. I just couldn't leave it, it looked so good for fertilising the croft."

'These days my nephew and I gather sheep up there. My nephew's always up there, and he says, "Well, John, every time I go past, I'm seeing Calum with the creel full of seaweed coming up."

'I remember going over to Arnish once, and meeting Calum, and he said, "John, a bhalaich, a calamity in the spring – I lost my cas-chrom, a bhalaich." I said, "What happened, what did you do? Did you use the spade instead?" And he said, "Oh, h-iarraidh, no. I spent two days looking around in the trees in Torran until I found one which had exactly the wood I needed, exactly what I wanted, a bhalaich." He built a new cas-chrom. He planed it, and dressed it, and everything. He said, "I wasn't too particular as long as it wasn't too rough where the hands went." '

There were more complex factors at work here than stubborn self-sufficiency. Calum MacLeod was displaying and embodying a deep belief in the capacities and qualities of a certain way of life in his small corner of the world. He would never lose that trust in his place and his people; he never faltered in his confidence that Gaelic resilience was adamantine, that Gaelic resourcefulness could move mountains and that the Gaelic language had evolved to describe miracles. Nothing more was needed. By sustaining that personal faith against all evidence and opposition he turned a great portion of it into truth. The intensity of his conviction would inform the smallest and the largest of his legacies.

He grew tobacco in Torran because, like carrying good seaweed on his back from the shore, or rebuilding his own cas-chrom, there was no good reason not to. "N am cogadh Hitler [at the time of Hitler's war]', he would tell the broadcaster Cailean Maclean in 1986, 'tobacco was getting scarce. Although I wasn't smoking, my father was a tobacco smoker and many of the neighbours round about were too.

'So we ordered six tobacco plants in the springtime. Before the plants arrived I got a basket of herring, and I put the guts of the herring on the tobacco plants. They grew, and they grew very well, and I was told not to let any slugs near them. If I didn't kill off the slugs, the slugs would eat them altogether.

'When the plants were my height I took off the leaves. They were like big dock leaves. They were eighteen inches long by four inches wide. When my father was at sea abroad, off America, he said he was getting the tobacco leaves very cheaply. They would take them aboard ship and dry them off. They were soaking them in rum or treacle and then rolling them up to dry, hanging off ropes. They would hang the soaked, rolled tobacco up for a few months until it was well seasoned before it would be opened. They were then opening it and smoking it as they needed to.

'When the leaves were ready I did exactly the same as my father said – when they were dry enough I put rum or treacle on them. When they were matured I gave them to my father, and he said it was the best tobacco he'd ever had. It was nice and light and there wasn't the same black oil in it as his usual tobacco.'*

In 1947 Calum's retainer from the Northern Lighthouse Board was both consolidated and increased. The Graham family had left Torran, and Calum MacLeod was made boatman-in-charge of the Rona lighthouse attending vessel. In 1950 Lexie MacLeod gave birth to a baby girl at Broadford Hospital in Skye. She was christened Julia, after Calum's mother. When Julia MacLeod was six months old the new, young family moved into Calum's grandfather's house at Arnish.

This crofthouse had originally been thatched, but in the twentieth century it was reroofed by Calum's grandfather with corrugated zinc sheets from the Raasay Estate's redundant pheasant hatchery. It faced, across a hundred yards of good croftland in a shallow, small and sheltered glen, the home of Calum's mother and father. It was a place of peace and beauty. It would become in time the last redoubt of the human civilisation of northern Raasay.

In the Hebridean context, a mains electricity supply arrived early in southern Raasay. On 29 October 1954

* Lexie and Calum's success with *Nicotiana tabacum* is less surprising in the light of the fact that Calum was an extremely skilled and productive agriculturalist. He devoted his own garden not only to fruit trees and root vegetables, but also to lettuce and other such native American species as tomatoes and courgettes. He personally disliked tomatoes and was not sure what to do with courgettes, until both were used by his wife in her celebrated variety of homemade chutney. Spare lettuces were offered to the cows, who rejected them.

a letter arrived at Inverness County Council from the secretary of the North of Scotland Hydro-Electric Board. The letter stated that 'some time ago it had been decided to lay a submarine cable from Skye to Raasay, to give supplies in the vicinity of Inverarish.

'Recently it had been decided to extend the distribution to the south of the Island and as far north as Balmeanach, so that electricity would be available to 134 potential consumers on the Island and only a few in the north would not be catered for.'

'. . . only a few in the north would not be catered for'.

Inverness County Council 'agreed to note the position with satisfaction'.

Calum MacLeod decided to generate his own electricity.

Winter nights are long in the Hebrides. Calum MacLeod's outdoor work between November and February would necessarily come to an end when he would bring in the cows from pasture as early as 3.30 or 4.00 p.m. After that, said his daughter, 'well, the [battery-powered] wireless was very much part of our life.

'We had to listen to the broadcasts from the lighthouse in Rona to the shore station at Portree, as well as to the daily shipping forecast. If there was any problem, my father might have to gather up his crew and go out. We needed the wireless because we had no phone – there was a phone box at what is now the upper car park, a few hundred yards away and it could ring forever, but nobody was there to hear it. So he had to listen to the lighthouse broadcast. I think that was twice a day. We listened to this daily broadcast from the rock and we took great interest in this. Then there was the news. Mealtimes were timed with the news. Lunch was one o'clock to coincide with the one o'clock news, and the evening meal was at six o'clock to fit in with the six o'clock news.'

Throughout his life, Calum MacLeod read voraciously and eclectically. Along with all of his neighbours in the north, and those in the south of Raasay until their mains electricity arrived in the 1950s, he did so during the winter nights by the light of a Tilley lamp. His household heat came from the peat-fired solid-fuel cooking stove,* and both heat and light were delivered by the paraffin-fired Tilley Storm Lamp which had been a feature of Highland and Hebridean homes since it was first put on the market in the 1920s. (Tilley also manufactured a popular paraffin laundry iron.)

But, if electricity, as well as tarmacadamed motor roads, was the coming thing in southern Raasay, Calum saw no reason why – even if the Hydro-Electric Board as well as Inverness County Council declined to cater for those 'few in the north' – Arnish should not also benefit from its own supply.

* Like many a Highlander and Hebridean of his and other generations, Calum MacLeod refused to countenance burning coal. It was not only a question of coal costing money while peat was freely cut from the hill. 'Dad hated coal,' said his daughter. 'Black dust, dense smoke, large fire-rakings – coal was no match for the fragrant peat smoke.'

Wind turbines, which fifty years later would become a
source of headline controversy in the Highlands and
Islands, were an infant technology in the early 1950s. It is
difficult to know which variety Calum MacLeod located
and installed.* But it was about the height of a telegraph
pole, and it had vanes, accumulators and batteries. He
erected it in the garden and – some of the time – it
powered bulbs in the hallway, the kitchen, the living
room, and a large window-light in the front porch.

For a while then, said Julia MacLeod, 'with our
electric light we were the bee's knees. But it had its
own sting in the tail. My father discovered that the
electric light was not so good as the Tilley – you didn't
get the same heat off it. And if it was going to get too
stormy you had to shut down the vanes in case they
spun off.

'The final crunch came when he had six weeks of flat
calm and frosty weather. There was no wind, not a

---

* His daughter Julia remembered the apparatus as a 'Lucas
Freelight Windmill'. It seems likely that Calum bought one of
the first small electrical-output wind turbines, which had become
popular at homesteads in the American Midwest, and which
simply used modified propellers, or vanes, to drive direct-current
generators. By the middle of the 1920s one- to three-kilowatt wind
generators had been developed by American companies such as
Parris-Dunn and Jacobs Wind-electric. These systems were only
installed at first to provide lighting for remote farms, and to charge
batteries used to power crystal radio sets. Their use was later
extended to an array of direct-current motor-driven appliances,
including refrigerators, freezers, washing machines and power
tools. But that would be rather too late for Calum – or more
relevantly, in the case of washing machines and refrigerators,
Lexie – MacLeod. They eventually settled for a paraffin fridge.

breath, and everything went flat. And everybody else in the neighbourhood said, "Well, our Tilley's still going!" So he went outside and chopped the windmill down and turned it into firewood.

'He reverted to the Tilley lamp until the calor gas canisters came in – you get a bit of heat off calor gas. He never had any other form of electricity generator. It was always just the Tilley and the stove, and then the calor light and gas stove.

'Oh – and in 1957 he took up recreational knitting. He bought a Knitmaster machine and made intricate Fair Isle patterns – sweaters, gloves and socks, which mother grafted in the final make-up.'

Between 1949 and 1952 Calum MacLeod built his first, albeit minor, roadway in the north of Raasay. The track to Fladda, where three families comprising twelve people still lived in 1951, as well as being in the usual sorry condition, had never been more than a side line heading west off the main Torran to Kyle Rona path. The quicker and more obvious route was to run a footway around the mile of coast between Torran and the Fladda narrows.

'Fladda was just served by a branch of the road going to Kyle Rona,' said Calum's brother Charles. 'At about a mile and a half up that track, there's a branch going down to Fladda. I can still pick it out among the heather and the rocks. But it was very inconvenient, of course, for the Fladda people. I reckon the council decided in about 1949 they would just make a track, a footpath, directly along the shore.

'They had only small sums of money available – I think about three sums of £70 [roughly £1,700 in today's terms] a year in all. But £70 would go a long way at that time. And we were paid by the hour, I think, when we started it off. Calum had been looking after the earlier footpath for years. The roads surveyor came along, and he just showed us roughly the way they wanted the track made through Torran straight on to Fladda.

'It started at the old mission building at Torran, and Calum and I worked there for three winters, I think we started in 1949, that would be 1949/50, 1950/51 and 1951/52, three winters. And each year we got £70, or £35 each, so the track cost £210. Which was not so bad for us in 1950. In 1950, one pound would go a long way.

'There had been a rough track going through Torran but we improved that, we widened it a bit, to about three foot wide. It couldn't take a cart, the actual path being only about three foot wide. But you had a grass verge on each side, probably a foot, so we would have to clear an area about five foot wide.

'We put some hard stuff in the middle and you had a grass verge of about a foot on each side, where that was possible – in some places it wouldn't work because there were too many rocks. It wasn't too bad when we left it and for years after that was used a lot and was very passable.'

John Nicolson of Torran would consider the Torran to Fladda coastal route to be one of the MacLeod family's unsung achievements. 'Everybody's all talking about Calum's road from Brochel to Arnish,' he said, 'and what a terrific feat, right enough, and everybody agrees about that. But I think something that people have forgotten about is that Calum engineered the road from the schoolhouse in Torran to Fladda.

'I wasn't at home at the time, but he and his brother Charles made that road. The roads engineer in Skye at the time, he went over, and they walked where the path is today between the schoolhouse in Torran and Fladda and his comment to Calum was, "If you can make a road there, you're welcome to carry on with it!" And he gave them an estimate of what it would cost.

'That track itself was a feat, when you look at the terrain that they were going through. Although they were only making a footpath there, it was even worse than the land he had to cross from Brochel Castle to Arnish. He and Charles engineered and made it themselves, and that path today [2005] is very nearly as good – except in one or two places where the rain has got the better of it because the drains haven't been kept cleaned and nobody is looking after it – it is nearly as good as the day it was made. A lot of people don't know about this, because the road from Brochel Castle to Arnish overshadowed everything else that Calum did.'

Calum MacLeod was firefighting the decline of northern Raasay with buckets and a hand-pump. Subsidising his new footpath between Torran and

Fladda was no more than a rare conciliatory gesture by Inverness County Council. In October 1950 the Department of Agriculture, as Raasay's state landlord was then known, 'intimated to Inverness County Council that they were prepared to undertake the widening and diversion of a section of the road and footpath between Brochel and Tarbet [half a mile south of Arnish]. The future maintenance of the road and footpath would be the responsibility of the local authority and the number of people to be served would be approximately 30.' But the county surveyor recommended to the county's roads committee that 'this road and footpath be not taken over as a Public Highway', and the roads committee happily agreed.

At the same meeting in Inverness the county council was also presented with yet another petition requesting a short footbridge to Fladda. It met the same fate as so many of its predecessors. It was volleyed with unreturnable force back to the district committee in Skye and was never heard of again.

Twelve years later, in 1962, Calum MacLeod himself raised with the local authority the possibility of a Fladda causeway. Lieutenant Colonel Neil McLean, DSO, MP, replied from the Scottish Office in London that 'The Engineer who visited Fladda in this connection has now reported that some 1,500 cubic yards of rock would have to be put down to ensure that the crossing could be made by foot at all states of the tide and he estimates the cost of the work at £2 10s to £3 per cubic yard [around £35 to £40]. This means that the total cost would certainly equal and perhaps exceed that of a foot bridge and we have already felt obliged to dismiss the latter project because of the prohibitive cost in relation to use.'

The prospect of land, electricity, public services and paid work in southern Raasay – where in the 1950s a forestry plantation scheme was started – Skye and further afield leached away the people of Fladda, Kyle Rona, Torran and Arnish. That two-mile hiatus of empty moorland and peat bog between Brochel Castle and Arnish loomed like a canyon between the future and the past. 'After the Second World War', said John Nicolson of Torran, 'people came back. We all came home, most of us came home after the war. And I reckon myself that, if there had been a road or a road was in the offing when the boys came home, things could have been a lot better in the north end of Raasay.'

Ironically, it was the same North of Scotland Hydro-Electric Board that refused to connect northern Raasay to the national grid which gave John Nicolson his first job away from Torran: 'After I got demobbed, in '47, I came home to Raasay, to Torran. My father was alive then, and my mother, and Alec, my brother. So I worked on the croft for that summer, giving everybody a hand, the same as I did before I ever went away. And I stayed at home for August and September after the harvest – and then I went away to work on the Hydro schemes in Glen Affric.

'After that I joined the lighthouse service in Orkney,

and I then came back to Portree in Skye. I think it was around then that I began to be aware of some chronic decline in the north of Raasay. My own father died, and you then start to think, "What's going to happen now?" I knew fine that the tradition was in the old days that the oldest person in the family got the croft, so I didn't have a look in really. So after I got demobbed, I got married and went away. I knew fine, that was me finished as far as the croft was concerned, unless we could get another one. And there was no work. There was no other work.'

John's older brother Murdo returned from the prison camp Stalag AB at the end of the war and in 1948 married a woman named Jessie MacLeod from Balachuirn in central Raasay. Murdo Nicolson also joined the lighthouse service, working at Cape Wrath and the Rona light until Murdo's father died in 1954 and Murdo and his wife Jessie moved back to the family's Torran croft. Their return with a school-aged boy revived Torran School, which had been closed due to an absence of pupils. Lexie MacLeod had been tutoring her young daughter Julia at home in Arnish, but when the family of Murdo and Jessie Nicolson arrived the education department of Inverness County Council re-employed Calum's wife as schoolmistress, and in November 1955 they opened the schoolroom doors once more.

'We started off with two of us,' said Julia MacLeod Allan, 'and the most pupils that were there in my time, up until 1962, was four. It was mostly part-time education, something like ten a.m. until one p.m., but when there were the four of us it went on until three o'clock – with breaks.' Jessie Nicolson would bring up four boys, and the youngest two would also be the last students to be taught by Lexie MacLeod, or anybody else, at Torran School.

For a short time in the 1950s the situation in this fragile, neglected peninsula seemed once again to stabilise. There were three families totalling twelve people occupying three houses in Fladda. There was Murdo and Jessie Nicolson and their sons in Torran, as well as Murdo's widowed mother and his brother Alec. The schoolhouse there was inhabited by Murdo Nicolson's sister Chrissie, her husband and her brother-in-law. There were three houses in Arnish, one of them occupied by Calum, Lexie and Julia MacLeod, another by Calum's parents, Donald and Julia, and his brother and sister Charles and Bella, and the third, on the brae of North Arnish, by their MacLeod cousins, a family of five.

'It wasn't really all that quiet a life,' said Jessie Nicolson. 'Not really – there was always somebody coming and going, especially as we were in between the two villages of Fladda and Arnish. There was always somebody calling. And of course, you're busy when you're bringing up four boys in a dangerous place like Torran. It's not an easy life, and you couldn't relax because it was dangerous with the rocks and being so near the seashore. Of course, when we got them to bed at night, that's when the work was done.

There was no television, but we had the radio right enough. Och, it was great – we were quite happy. Nobody moaned or complained. We just took everything in our stride. We were happy with our own wee world, as you might say.'

In 1958 the MacLeod family left North Arnish for Eyre in the deep south of Raasay, reducing at a stroke the north's population by a further 17 per cent to twenty-four people. They had run the small local post office, and after their departure that franchise was passed on to Jessie and Murdo Nicolson in Torran. Calum MacLeod was by then the only postman serving northern Raasay, collecting the mailbag three times a week from a mail van at Brochel, carrying it on his shoulder along the broken footpath to be sorted at Torran, and then delivering to Fladda and to his family at Arnish.*

Conversations over the parcel- and envelope-sort at Torran post office were possibly unique in the annals of the Royal Mail. 'Calum took so much interest in what had happened on the island in the past,' said Jessie Nicolson. 'The history of Raasay, you know – he could go back to when Raasay was in private hands – when a Mr Wood had Raasay, and he had stories about Rainy too, about what a bad, ruthless factor he had. Very interesting stories like that. I'm sorry now

---

* Calum would later recall that his first wages from the post office were deducted to the tune of 7s 6d a week to pay off a £100 loan from the Fisheries Board, which he had borrowed to buy 'lin falmair', or hake nets, in the 1930s before prices tumbled and he abandoned fishing as a livelihood.

that I didn't pay more attention. But this was what we used to talk about, when we had the post office, when we were getting the Fladda mail sorted – this was the conversation most of the time: the nineteenth century and Rainy and Wood, while we were sorting the mail-order clothes for Fladda. Nice times to look back on, very nice times to think back on.'

Apart from the postal delivery and one or two courtings, the north remained as separated from the south of Raasay in the 1950s as when the landowner Rainy had built his wall almost a century earlier. The north, with that wasteland between its crofts and the adopted road at Brochel, looked instead westward, over the water to Skye. 'As far as the north end and the south end of Raasay were concerned', said John Nicolson, 'they were two different places. The fishing boats from the north end of Raasay went to Portree. We got all our stores from Portree. The only time you went to the south end to get stores was if it was bad weather and you couldn't get to Portree – more often than not it would be to get tobacco for the old folk, because being without tobacco was worse than being in jail!'

The administrative and shopping centre of Portree in Skye was five sea miles from Loch Arnish. Calum MacLeod's job as boatman to the Rona light required him to ferry the keepers to and from Skye and Rona every two weeks to work their staggered, overlapping shifts. He had also to keep them in supplies, which enabled him also to pick up the shopping for the north of Raasay. 'We got all our supplies from Portree,' said

Jessie Nicolson. 'Calum had the lighthouse boat, and we got all our supplies from Portree, we had no dealings with the south end. We used to say "the north end doesn't belong to the south end!" The lighthouse boat was our lifeline. Calum would bring over everything that we needed really. We posted our orders over to the shopkeepers in Portree, and Calum and Donald and Calum Tom from Fladda, or whoever was available, they collected our groceries for us. And then you had to improvise, you know, make do with lots of things.'

This maritime provision of supplies to the district was a lengthy process which was undertaken at all times of year and in most weather conditions. It was more than a quick hop across the Sound of Raasay. A typical run might involve the boat in a one-hour voyage from the Fladda narrows to Portree, then a two-hour crossing to Rona, then a two-hour return to Portree, concluded by another one-hour return to Fladda and Loch Arnish. At every stage, of course, men and supplies had to be embarked and unloaded.

'There were three men on Rona,' Julia MacLeod Allan explained. 'They were there for four weeks on, two weeks off, and my father would take the new person out from Portree with all the gear that went out to the lighthouse. He would go from Portree to Rona, take the "going home" lightkeeper back to Portree, collect our provisions and bring them back into Loch Arnish, drop them off into the dinghy there, and then drop the rest off in Fladda. So, we got that every fortnight, weather permitting – and the Portree merchants J. & R. MacLeod permitting, Malcolm Gillies permitting, Lipton permitting! Mother used to write wee things like "or nearest" on the order, because if it didn't come, you were stuck, with no alternative. If you were wanting strawberry jelly, for instance, you would have to add "or nearest", because you wanted some jelly even if it wasn't strawberry. Any jelly is better than no jelly! She also had an account with the department store Copland and Lyle in Sauchiehall Street, Glasgow. Copland's was probably the equivalent of . . . Harrods is maybe pushing it a little bit, but it was quite "up there".

'Dad was always on the go,' continued his daughter, 'always rushing hither and thither when the time and weather allowed. He took things personally; he took everything to heart; he saw almost everything as his own responsibility. Because of their croft and animal commitments, Mum and he could not holiday together. Dad usually went to Nigg on the north-east coast and stayed there with his brother Ronald. He saw more marvels between Raasay and Nigg than others did when travelling the world! And collecting various boats for the Northern Lighthouse Board took him to places such as Barra in the Outer Hebrides and Macduff in Banff.

'I remember that at Macduff he was held up while technicians worked on his boat, the *Janet Mackenzie*. She was moored alongside several fishing boats and he had to cross over many decks to get to the harbourside

and his hotel and his cups of tea. The fishery crews
were so nice and chatty – but, mysteriously, none of
them offered him a cup of tea. Only later did he
discover that they were all Closed Brethren.'*

The insularity of northern Raasay had, since the
nineteenth century, been bolstered by the fact that its
children got all of their schooling at Torran. Before the
Second World War a standard regimen applied to all
small rural state schools, instructing and enabling
them to supply a basic all-subject junior/secondary
education to scholars between the ages of five and
fourteen years. There was a possibility of a fuller term
of secondary education, but for many it was a very
remote possibility indeed.

In the Highlands and Islands of Scotland only some
towns offered that extended secondary education.
After 1918 travelling expenses or a lodging allowance
became available for pupils from remote areas who
had passed the examination qualifying them for secondary education, and some children could also apply

* The Closed, or Exclusive, or Darbyite Brethren are a splinter
of the Plymouth Brethren, a Protestant Nonconformist group
founded in 1827. The Open Plymouth Brethren are prepared to
share a communion table with other, unaffiliated Christians.
The Closed Brethren are not prepared to do so. The Closed
Brethren attracted a following in the fishing ports of north-
eastern Scotland, where as late as 2002 a visitor to Fraserburgh,
just twenty miles from Macduff, discovered that 'members of
the Closed Brethren still serve tea in a separate room for guests
who are not of the faith'. There would not, presumably, have
been a separate room in which to offer Calum MacLeod tea
on the otherwise friendly fishing boats which he encountered
in Macduff.

for a bursary. To accommodate those children residential school hostels were built in such parishes as Dingwall, Inverness, Golspie, Dornoch, Fort William . . . and Portree in Skye.

'When we came to twelve years of age', said John Nicolson, 'the qualifying papers arrived at the school, and you had to pass the qualifying before you went to Portree High School. Now, all the time that I was in Torran School, there was only one person that went to Portree and that was Sheila Cumming, who was in the same class as myself. You needed to go for a grant, and to go and ask for anything like that in my young days was unthought of . . . if my father or anyone asked for money! Oh gosh me, that was the last thing on earth you'd do – to go to ask anybody to help you. It was hard enough for them to go to the bank to get five pounds or ten pounds to buy herring nets or other things they needed for their livelihood. But to go and send me or anybody else to Portree to get their education . . . no!'

By the time that Calum and Lexie MacLeod's daughter, Julia, reached the age of twelve at Torran School, legislation had changed. The 1945 Education Act (Scotland) had raised the school leaving age to fifteen years, the last three or more years of which were to be served in a specialised secondary school. That additional tier of tutelage was both free of charge and compulsory.

And so in 1962 Julia MacLeod 'got a letter saying, "Thou shalt have two skirts, four blouses, one tie, one dressing gown . . . And so when I was twelve all that was packed in a trunk and shipped off to Portree High School, along with me.' She was dismally unhappy: 'I'll never get over the move to Portree, it was awful. I don't think anyone is ready at twelve to sever all ties. I became one of sixty-seven girls, having been the only girl in school all through my primary.' Julia's misery at being wrenched from the small, Gaelic-speaking extended family of northern Raasay, transferred from part-time to full-time education and tipped into a crowded, suburban, impersonal, rowdy, entirely unfamiliar and often Anglophone school was compounded by the fact that she was hardly ever able to get back to Arnish. The Caledonian MacBrayne steamer timetables did not offer a daily crossing between Skye and Raasay, and nor was one provided on Friday night and Monday morning. Her predicament was complicated further by the absence of a motor road between Brochel and her home.

At the start of their holidays a car would taxi Julia MacLeod and a succession of the Nicolson boys from the ferry pier in southern Raasay up to Brochel, where they would be met by parents and from where they would walk. Even that arrangement could break down. On one occasion in winter a heavy snowfall blocked the adopted road, and Julia and her schoolmates were left on the high moor south of Glame, some miles from Brochel and even further from South Arnish. The children walked northwards with their suitcases before seeking shelter in the lee of a rock, because the snow had obscured the margins of the open road, and because they understood the mortal danger of losing their bearings in a blizzard. They were discovered there some hours later by Calum MacLeod.

Julia was boarded in the Margaret Carnegie Hostel for Girls in Portree for the whole of her secondary years, except for school holidays and occasional long weekends. She had effectively, at the age of twelve, left home. Julia MacLeod would never return to live in northern Raasay. 'You were taken away at twelve,' she said, 'and you left school to do something else, somewhere else. I mean, what would you come back and do in Arnish? Milk half of the cow – let your father milk the other half? What would you do? I remember my mother said we should have a chinchilla farm – she was desperately trying to think of what would make money and provide us with a livelihood. I did try to crew the *Janet Mackenzie* with my father, but catching mooring buoys and climbing perpendicular pier ladders were beyond my abilities!'

Calum MacLeod never forgave the state for removing his only child. His life's experience had taught him to cherish what was independent and peripheral and to mistrust centralised authority. That mistrust would in the following years veer towards hatred.

Eleven years after Julia's departure for Portree, Calum prepared an article on 'The Ruination of Raasay' for the *West Highland Free Press*. 'Another factor that caused bitter discontent', he wrote as the days began to shorten in the September of 1973, 'and

added to the depopulation of the island is the tyrannous system of centralised education pursued by the
Scottish Education Department during the last two
decades.

'In practice, this form of education compels every
pupil on attaining 11½ years of age to leave home and
be boarded elsewhere for the rest of their education –
about 4½ years. The result is that homes in rural areas
are systematically emptied and, in fact, all rural areas
and especially the islands reduced to a skeleton of
aging population while villages and towns are
crammed by youngsters outwith parental supervision
and growing up urbanised to such an extent that they
become practically alien to home environments or
participating in agriculture or fishing. In fact, indus-
trial or manual work is frowned on, while moral
delinquency, especially immorality, vandalism and
drinking has increased to an unprecedented scale. This
moral rot with a major decline in teaching and especially lack of training for future citizenship is simply
due to the policy pursued by the Scottish Education
Department.

'A tourist that saw the system in operation in Suther-
land – children removed by buses for nearly 100 miles
from homes, on poor roads, in inclement weather, and
brought up compulsorily amidst permissive environments – described it as "the most devilish system of
education I have ever seen in my worldwide travels".

'Such has been the system of education forced on
Raasay during the last two decades. It was rigorously

enforced by Inverness Education Authority as represented by Dr J. A. MacLean and his depute, Mr Lawson. Before me lie their worthless written assurances to parents regarding children so removed. To quote a few – "Children so removed will be well cared for." "With children so removed progress educationally is most remarkable, and marvellous in sociableness and poise." "In their best interests to attend Portree High School."

'. . . Raasay has been ruined by the gross maladministration (if not criminal) of St Andrews House [the Scottish Office], and the gross negligence of Inverness County Council, and by the tyrannous system of education advocated by the Scottish Office, and rigorously pursued by the county's Director of Education – Dr J. A. MacLean, and his depute, Mr Lawson – heirs typical of the infamous Loch and Sellar* – of the former century – harassing and driving their less fortunate fellow-countrymen out of their homes.'

Expressing his ire in the columns of local newspapers was both catharsis and a form of revenge for Calum MacLeod. But it would not bring his daughter or his community home. And this was a restless,

---

* Calum was referring here to James Loch and Patrick Sellar, the Scottish commissioner and factor respectively of Lord Stafford's immense Sutherlandshire estate in the 1810s. Loch and Sellar enforced the wholesale and frequently brutal removal of the estate's tenants to make space for sheep-farming, and have been accused of seminal responsibility for the institutionalised clearances that affected the north and west of Scotland for much of the rest of the nineteenth century.

physically active man. He needed to do something that was solid and practical and equally shaming to the authorities.

So, at some uncertain point in the 1960s, he decided to build the road from Brochel Castle to South Arnish himself.

No Chance of Being
Run Down by a Car

The tools which each foreman roadman should have
are a shovel, spade, line and reel, pickaxe, barrow and
a hand-machine scraper.

Thomas Aitken, *Road Making
and Maintenance*, 1900

It is difficult to be sure in which year – let alone which
month, week or day – Calum MacLeod began first to
build Calum's road.

John Nicolson of Torran, who was by then living
in Skye but who returned regularly to the north end
of Raasay, thought that it was as early as the 1950s:
'In the '50s you were seeing that Calum was doing
things to the road. When you leave Brochel Castle,
and the road goes right up near the top – he'd
started making a road below that. That's when
we became aware of it first. And in other places,
where the road was going down steep braes, he was
making detours, and I suppose it was after I moved

back to Skye in 1954 that we realised what he was trying to do.'

Calum's daughter Julia said, 'I think he started in 1962. I think it was the sheer frustration of me having to go to Portree that made him begin it.'

Calum himself told the *West Highland Free Press* in August 1975 that he had worked on the road from plans drawn up 'eight years ago', in 1967. He would tell the same newspaper in 1979 that he had commenced road-building in 1964. He repeated the year 1964 to the *Scotsman* in 1980. He told the journalists Magnus Magnusson in 1982 and Tom Weir in 1986 that he had started in 1966. Colonel Basil Reckitt's Raasay journal records him as starting in 1965. In 1973, following a meeting in Raasay with Calum MacLeod, the broadcaster Derek Cooper reported that Calum 'began to convert this track into a road . . . four years ago', in 1969 . . .

Much of the confusion is explicable, and has little to do with Hebridean disregard for the precise recording of time. As the local postman, Calum had to walk the old track every other day. As a crofter, his family's peat-cutting was at one side of it, closer to Brochel than to Arnish. As a father, his only child was boarding in Portree and depended upon the pathway to get home at all. So Calum MacLeod maintained the track between Brochel and Arnish for many years when it was in his interest to do so, and there may be a fine line between watching a man maintain a track, and watching a man in the first stages of turning that track into a twelve-foot-wide roadway.

There is also a fine line between planning something and beginning to put the plan into effect. It is certain that Calum MacLeod had thought long and hard for very many years about a road between Arnish and Brochel. He was a practical man. His experience in engineering the Torran to Fladda coastal footway, and his even greater experience of walking between Brochel and Arnish, had afforded him both the qualifications and the opportunity to work out how such a road could be built. He and his brother Charles had been told that the path to Fladda would be a difficult if not impossible task. But they had built it. By later in the 1950s and into the 1960s Calum MacLeod was being told by Inverness County Council's officials 'that £30,000 [equivalent to £450,000 today] at least would be spent before any vehicle could cross these 3,000 yards' between Brochel Castle and Arnish.

How, considered the man who had built the Fladda track himself, could they have come to such an absurd conclusion?

He bought a book. It was an obvious book to buy. For half a crown (or two shillings and sixpence, or twelve and a half pence, or approximately two pounds in twenty-first-century value), Calum got hold of a hardback original of *Road Making and Maintenance: A Practical Treatise for Engineers, Surveyors, and*

Others, which had been published in 1900 by Thomas
Aitken.*

Aitken's great book was a DIY manual to building
motor-ways where motor-ways had not previously
existed. It was intended as a guide to every rung on
the road-building ladder, from surveyor to engineer to
foreman to gang, and as Calum MacLeod intended to
be his own surveyor, engineer, foreman and gang
virtually every chapter was relevant and instructive.
Turning absorbedly through its 440 pages, Calum will
have alighted on two especially encouraging passages.
'The width of a new road', observed Thomas Aitken,
'will be determined by the prospective wheel traffic. It
is a common practice to make a road sufficiently wide
to allow of two or more vehicles passing each other
easily when travelling fast. For ordinary road traffic 12
feet of metalling will be sufficient.'

Calum did not anticipate extraordinary road traffic
between Brochel and Arnish. The road he planned
would be twelve feet in total width and nine feet
wide within its outer drains and dry-stone edges.
In order to achieve this, 'the tools which each foreman roadman should have', wrote Thomas Aitken,

---

* Aitken, a native of Cupar in Fife, was in 1900 the president of
the Road Surveyors' Association of Scotland. He would gain
international renown as a consulting roads engineer at the beginning of the age of the motorcar. In 1907 he won a hundred-guinea
prize from the British Roads Improvement Association for 'Aitken's Pneumatic Tar Sprayer', a machine invented to prevent dust
clouds from rising on dry summer roads used by motorcars, and
in 1911 he was attracted to Delaware in the USA to advise on the
construction of a statewide highway.

'are a shovel, spade, line and reel, pickaxe, barrow and a hand-machine scraper'. A shovel, spade, line and reel, pickaxe and barrow were easily supplied. Upon further reading the hand-machine scraper turned out to be unnecessary in the short term, it being a device for cleaning and clearing the finished surface.

Calum requested the assistance of two officers of the Royal Engineers in surveying the lines of the new road. Major Mitcham and Captain Harrison duly arrived in Raasay and the three men staked out a route between Brochel and Arnish. 'After the war', said John Nicolson, 'the army were helping people like that in different places. "Aid to the Community", it was called.* And they were going to do Calum's road, before he began it himself. It was even pegged out. He pegged it out along with the army engineers who came there. He showed them where it should go, more or less following the road as it is today. A stop was put to it after that, as far as I can understand, by certain members of Inverness County Council.'

'The Royal Engineers were going to do the road in the 1960s,' said Calum MacLeod in 1979. 'But the old Lord Macdonald caused trouble.† He was convener of

* Military Aid to the Civil Community (MACC) is an essential and ongoing domestic responsibility of the British armed forces. It is loosely defined as 'providing Service personnel and equipment, in both emergencies and routine situations, to assist the community at large'.
† 7th Lord Macdonald and High Chief of Clan Donald was a major hereditary landowner in Skye, although not in Raasay. Between 1932 and his death in 1970 he was also a central figure on Inverness County Council, of which he became vice-convener in 1952 and full convener in 1968. For most of the postwar years he was also chairman of the council's roads committee.

this and convener of that [on Inverness County Council]. Wherever you turned, he was in the way. He diverted the Royal Engineers and had them build instead some track in the Cuillins that nobody ever used.'

Major Mitcham, Captain Harrison and Calum MacLeod at least managed to get most of the road planned before the enforced military withdrawal. And they did so according to the precepts of Thomas Aitken. 'The selection or location of country roads', advised Aitken, 'is carried out by making an examination or reconnaissance of the tract of country to be traversed, so as to obtain the requisite data for the purpose of determining the best route and gradients for the proposed line of communication.'

Calum MacLeod had been making that examination or reconnaissance for the best part of half a century.

'The most direct or shortest practicable route between two points at once suggests itself,' continued Aitken, 'but this, in every case, must be governed by the natural features of the surface of the country. The object aimed at is to ascertain the most favourable direction in which to lay out a road, so as to convey the traffic with the least amount of motive power consistent with reasonable economy in construction and in the subsequent maintenance of the road and works.'

Those words chimed perfectly with Calum's philosophy, as already established: 'If Calum was doing anything, he didn't do it the hard way. If there was an easy way, he did it the easy way . . . He looked at the contours of the land, and the surface of the ground, and if they meant going down a certain way, and it was easier than cutting up another way, that's the way Calum would go. The hard way may have looked shorter, but it might still have been harder to do – so he would dig a wee turn.'

Aitken noted helpfully that 'existing roads . . . in hilly districts in most parts of the country, have to a great extent been laid down with only one object in view, namely, that of a direct line. The great sacrifice thus entailed, through steep gradients, in the cost of transportation, is a serious one, which could have been avoided in many cases by a little scientific knowledge of what is necessary in laying out a new road, so as to accomplish the greatest amount of work in haulage at the least expenditure of motive power.'

In other words, roads which ran straight up a steep gradient were delusory. They looked quicker and cheaper, but they were not. A gentle, winding slope over twice the distance was actually more efficient. And there was another factor: 'A sinuous course is in most cases a decided advantage, from a maintenance point of view, as on a winding road the wheel traffic spreads over the whole surface, which seldom takes place on a straight road.'

Messrs MacLeod, Mitcham and Harrison had little difficulty in staking out the recommended sinuous course between Brochel and Arnish. The terrain demanded that they either go around outcrops of granite the size of a banqueting table or blow them up, and in most cases they preferred to skirt them.

But at certain points something more than sinuosity was required. At about halfway along the route the old track had encountered a steep-sided glen. This defile ran from east coast to west. Its southern slopes were difficult; its northern slopes were almost inaccessible. So the old track had run straight down the side of the southern slope, crossed the narrow, flat bottom, and then followed the foot of the northern slope down to the seashore at Loch Arnish.

Calum MacLeod probably did not need Thomas Aitken or officers of the Royal Engineers to tell him that the route straight down the southern slope of the glen was not only inefficient for wheeled transport, it was arguably impassable. A lengthy diversion was called for. He abandoned the old track altogether and laid out a massive dog-leg which ran firstly away from the western coast up the valley, and then down the other side towards Loch Arnish, casually picking up and tucking under its arm the residual track as it passed on its way to the sea. From there it would run around the placid side of Loch Arnish, where the few white houses of Torran came into view across the water on its northern bank, before wrestling through more birch trees and ascending a final hillside into the township of Arnish. He originally planned another short diversion, to the south of George Rainy's wall, but it was abandoned. His stone markings of this uncompleted detour still stand in the heather, remnants and evidence of those months of survey.

When the officers returned to barracks, Calum began to clear the land, to lay foundations, to build holding walls and culverts. A student at Duncan of Jordanstone College of Art in Dundee named Campbell Sandilands would in the early 1980s spend time with Calum MacLeod in order to write a dissertation on his road. In the early stages, Sandilands learned, Calum had 'by hand to make a "tram-line" of stones defining the finite boundary of the road. This was then filled in with more stones and then smaller stones between the larger ones . . . Gravel and small stones were quarried to complete the road surface.'

The arduous clearance of foliage by pick and shovel and wheelbarrow could not be limited to the roadway itself. 'It ought never to be forgotten', Thomas Aitken had written, 'that in order to have the surface of a road perfect, it must be kept completely dry . . . It is absolutely necessary to remove trees from the sides of the road . . . Not less than 20 per cent of the expense of repairing roads is incurred by the trees . . . keeping the road wet.'

This was the type of work, the first fifth of a mile of hard labour, that Basil Reckitt observed personally in April of 1966, noting in his journal that 'Calum MacLeod has been working on it for the last six months.' Calum had been toiling, then, through a period of what seemed to be a terminal crisis in the human affairs of northern Raasay. In 1964 the *Oban*

Times sent a photographer to the north end of Raasay, perhaps to record some rare surviving fragment of traditional Hebridean life. The newspaper later printed a selection of picturesque snaps and captions. 'Calum MacLeod, Arnish, the postman for North Raasay, approaching Fladda' was the caption beneath a landscape shot of Calum, complete with Wellington boots and postman's cap, a hefty, bulging canvas bag hanging from his right shoulder, strolling down the track towards the tidal narrows between Raasay and Fladda. The trim houses of Fladda are in the immediate distance, and Calum is, of course, walking along an extremely broad, flat and well-maintained stretch of coastal pathway: the pathway that he had built with his brother Charles thirteen years earlier.

Another photograph was captioned 'Provisions arrive off the lighthouse relief boat. The picture shows Fladda people and families home on holiday.' And there they stand, in a cheerful group close to the shore, facing piles of promising parcels: Katie MacKenzie (née Gillies), home from Gairloch on the mainland; James MacKenzie; Katie Gillies; Mary Gillies; Bella MacLeod; and Cathie MacAskill (née MacLeod), over from Struan in Skye. And in the middle of them, smiling indulgently, stands 'Calum MacLeod, postman and captain of the lighthouse boat but wearing lighthouse service cap'.

There were others photos: of Fladda men shearing sheep up by Kyle Rona, of the ladies of Fladda carrying their goods in wicker creels on their backs from the lighthouse boat up the hill to home, of husbands and wives and dogs on the hillside and outside their front door.

Shortly afterwards, at the end of the year, a small news item appeared in the *Oban Times*. 'With the closing of 1964', it read, 'a chapter in the history of the small islet of Fladda on the north-west coast of Raasay has come to an end . . . A few weeks ago, Mr and Mrs John Gillies moved from their home on the islet to Inverarish at the south end of Raasay.

'John Gillies, better known as "Iain Handy", is a well-known character in these parts and was often referred to as the "King of Fladda", having lived there for 50 years.

'Until last autumn three families lived on Fladda which is joined to the mainland of Raasay at low tide but is a mile by footpath to the next habitation (Torran and Arnish) and a further three miles [*sic*] by the same footpath from the end of the road leading to the south end of Raasay where the only shop on the island is – twelve miles from Fladda.

'Including Torran and Arnish a total of six families live at the north end of Raasay which at the time of the First World War supported nearly forty.

'But isolation has proved too much . . . it will not be very long before Fladda becomes deserted, and Torran and Arnish as well.'

The *Oban Times* was correct in its first two predictions. In 1965 the last families left Fladda. They and their parents and their grandparents had spent more than eighty years pleading for such basic services as a footbridge and a roadway. By the middle of the 1960s it was clear that the authorities had no intention of beginning to supply them with such commonplace late-twentieth-century amenities as electricity and running water. So they left for the modern world, in the south end of Raasay and beyond. The official census for Fladda in 1961 registered seven males and five females as resident in the island. In 1971, and thereafter, the Fladda census was returned as 'Nil'.

The house-of-cards effect on what remained of the rest of the north of Raasay was just as the *Oban Times* had suggested. 'Oh, it was terrible, it was terrible – awful when they left Fladda,' said Jessie Nicolson of Torran. 'You missed them, because you knew there was nobody going to visit you, and you weren't going to see anybody – in a small-knit community like that, you do miss them. And we did miss them, very much so. Very much so.'

Very quickly, almost all the remaining humanity of this small place left it for one destination or another. In 1966 Calum MacLeod's father, Donald, died. Donald MacLeod's mortal remains were taken out of Loch Arnish by his son Calum on the lighthouse boat. 'My father could hire the lighthouse boat for personal use – all he had to do was contact Edinburgh and they usually said "yes",' said Julia MacLeod Allan. 'On the day of my grandfather's funeral, my father had to go and get the lighthouse boat from Fladda and bring it round. They took the coffin down to the boat and set it on the boat and sailed it down to the south end. The men went to the cemetery, but women did not go. That is not the case now, but it was a tradition. The women went straight home.'

In the following year, 1967, Calum's mother Julia, his sister Bella and his brother Charles went to live at Portree in Skye. On 15 July 1967 the post office at Torran, a symbol of national recognition and identity which had stood on that remote shore since 1898, was shut down as Murdo and Jessie Nicolson and their family left for the mainland. With the post office closure went Calum MacLeod's part-time job as postman. In the same year the home anchorage of the Rona lighthouse relief boat was moved from Raasay to Portree. With the children, and apparently all prospect of future children, gone Torran School, which had first opened in 1839, was closed for good, and with it went Lexie MacLeod's job.

Suddenly – in the space of two years – there was nobody left in northern Raasay, Fladda and Eilean Tighe but the 56-year-old Calum and Lexie MacLeod of South Arnish. Adding insult to injury, the telephone manager from Aberdeen stepped in that autumn to remove the public telephone box at Arnish, 'as there would only be one householder remaining in the district, who had made application for a private tele-phone service'. 'My father only applied for a home telephone', said his daughter, 'after learning of the plan to remove the kiosk.'

It should have been endgame, and some thought that it was. They did not know Calum MacLeod. He raged against the dying of the light. His fury, which was far from evident to any casual acquaintance, found a number of expressions. 'Is it any wonder Scots emigrate?' he asked the correspondence columns of the *Stornoway Gazette* in April 1967, five years after Julia's departure for Portree and in the year of the depopulation of Torran and the closure of Torran School.

'The decline and fall of the system of education they prided in, and which was unsurpassed in excellency anywhere in the world, began with the closure and downgrading of the local one and two teacher schools, wherein was a high degree of individual tuition and responsibility. Unlike what we have now, seven teachers to one subject in four sessions, and staff changing like the Guards at Buckingham Palace, and children away from parental care at twelve years of age, devastating the Highlands and Islands.'

Three years later, in the last weeks of Harold Wilson's second Labour Government, Calum would give his enemy a political face. The detailed personal analysis of the decline and fall of northern Raasay – which was never named as such in his essay, but which was surely the spectral 'crofting community' at the heart of his thesis – laid the blame at the door of one particular creed. 'Socialism', he wrote to the *Stornoway Gazette* in May 1970, was responsible for 'remote authoritarian units that have no consideration for, and are mainly very ignorant of, local factors essential to benefit those concerned.

'During the last two decades, this system was pursued by its advocates in education, police, postal and transport facilities in rural areas and islands. The whole north-western seaboard of Britain – from Shetland in the north to Arran and Bute, including the Hebrides – were subjected to the downgrade system.

'First, rural schools were closed and pupils transported to or boarded at central schools in villages or towns as far as 100 miles from home. This was done amidst protests by parents whose families were broken up, and had the most devastating effect on small crofting communities, in most cases leading to total extinction. The Socialist Scottish Secretary makes much ado about the decline in emigration, but the bare truth is that in rural areas there are no Scots left to emigrate. To have under thirteen pupils in a rural school was "unrealistic", therefore it must be closed and the crofting community thereby destroyed . . .

'In this county alone about 70 rural schools were closed, with parents driven out of their homes to villages or cities. These transactions were going on under the very noses of the Crofters Commission and the Highland Development Board, and for all the help rendered by those bodies to crofters to prevent the tyranny, both would be as well dumped into the Moray Firth, along with their expensive offices around their necks.

'Next, the policing of rural areas as subjected to "centralisation" and amalgamated with those of county town, and policemen in crofting villages replaced by mobile units operated from elsewhere, which can never command the same respect. Besides, it meant the loss of another family to each locality – that had already lost their schoolteacher by the same system of administration.

'The Postal Service was the next to be "centralised". In rural areas offices were either closed or down-graded, and senior officers removed elsewhere. Thus another family was lost to the crofting community – a third family turned out of the area by the authorities, who undoubtedly foster depopulation without any worthwhile saving or gain, which is most destructive to the economy of these localities. Undoubtedly the Socialist "pet" has proved a devastating curse to the Highlands and Islands.'*

Like many another mild-mannered, naturally cour-teous and relatively shy man, Calum MacLeod was able to channel his anger into the written word. Unlike most others, he was also able to assuage it by building a road. The quick evaporation of the last populations

---

* This letter provoked an immediate and spirited response from Mrs Christina McFadden of the island of Barra. Mrs McFadden was a former member of Inverness County Council who, in the nature of most Hebridean representatives, stood some way to the political left of her mainland landowning colleagues. 'It was not under a Socialist government that the first forced emigration of our people began,' she chided Calum MacLeod. 'It was not under a Socialist government that island children had to bring peats to school to help warm them in wintry weather; carry a piece of bread, usually without butter or jam, for lunch; walk miles to school, often arriving cold and wet, the lunch piece already eaten; trudge back home, lucky if a meal awaited them . . .'

of Fladda and northern Raasay between 1964 and 1967 radically altered the purpose of the road. It would no longer assist in preserving his community. 'We were sorry that he didn't start a year or two earlier,' said Jessie Nicolson. 'Say, three or four years earlier – maybe we would have never left Torran, I don't know . . . it was coming too late to save the community.'

But if a road could no longer be used for the preservation of a population, it could encourage a revival. And there still was a population: a small one admittedly, of just two middle-aged people, but not to be despised for that. And at the very end of the day, of a life, or of a community, there was a statement to be made. It might, and would, be scorned as a pointless gesture, a Parthian shot, a quixotic tilt, a Pyrrhic victory. But any gesture, any shot or tilt, any victory was better than none at all.

Calum would not give up. He paused once, but only to clarify a point of law. Calum realised that the mineral rights to the island of Raasay belonged neither to himself nor – as was usual – to his crofting landlord, the Department of Agriculture. The mineral rights, which sixty years earlier had so excited the ironmasters William Baird & Co., had apparently been sold, along with Raasay House and several of the island's other important amenities, to a famously obstructive absentee speculator from Cooden in Sussex named Dr John Green. The very rocks which Calum MacLeod was blasting into shape in order to force an orderly route to the north end of Raasay were apparently, therefore, the property of a man (yet another man) whose only interest in the island was commercial. Luckily, said Calum, 'we discovered a loophole in the laws and were able to continue'.

'He was building the road because it would be of use to the people and it was of use to himself,' said Jessie Nicolson. 'So that he could get around and his wife could get out, you know. To my knowledge he never thought of giving up on it. And knowing Calum, Calum would not give up on it.'

'I don't think he ever considered giving it up,' said his daughter, Julia. 'His determination wouldn't let him think anything but, "I'm going to do this." He thought that the road would help with the repopulation of the north end. I think he's on the record as saying that – that it could bring work. Fish-farming, strangely enough, was something that he mentioned. And eventually, a fish farm came to the north of Raasay. I'm not sure how he would have felt about the actual fish farm – but he was broad-minded enough to accept that it was the price for progress.'

'Lexie wasn't well,' said John Nicolson. 'She had poor feet. Now, I heard Calum saying this myself:

' "Well, a bhalaich, the road, a bhalaich. I'll no finish, a bhalaich, until that road, a bhalaich, is at the back of the house and I can get my wife away in a car."

'He put that in front of himself, and he did carry on until he finished.'

In 1967 Calum MacLeod gained his lighthouse keeper's certificate and his job with the Northern Lighthouse Board was upgraded. He became the local assistant keeper on the Rona light.* He would keep this responsibility until the Rona lighthouse was automated in 1975. It required him to work for four weeks in Rona followed by two weeks at home. During that fortnight at home this man, who was then aged between fifty-six and sixty-four years, would complete his crofting chores: his animal husbandry – he had at one time as many as eighty sheep and fourteen cattle – his vegetable garden, his crops and his peat-cutting. He would also continue to build the motor road between Brochel Castle and Arnish.

In the latter, signature task he was not left entirely alone. His landlord, the Department of Agriculture and Fisheries for Scotland (DAFS), agreed to assist with the blasting necessary both to create aggregate and gravel for the road's foundations and rough surfacing, and to clear throughways through certain

* The job description of 'local assistant keeper' differed only from the standard 'assistant keeper' in that Calum MacLeod was employed by the NLB to work only on the Rona light: he could not be transferred to other stations. Donald MacSwan, who had been born in Rona at the turn of the twentieth century, returned there for a day trip in 1973 and later recounted how 'We walked up to the lighthouse – which is quite a climb – and there we were welcomed with great cordiality by the lighthouse keepers. They immediately made us a very welcoming cup of tea. They have very comfortable quarters there with electric fires, TV and all mod cons. The officer on duty – Malcolm MacLeod (a relief keeper from Arnish, Raasay) – showed us over the lighthouse, explaining how everything was done and how the light itself operated.'

patches of granite that could not be removed by hand with a pickaxe. The Engineering Department of the Department of Agriculture provided a compressor, explosives, a driller and a blaster. DAFS then subcontracted – and paid – the local county roads department in Portree to second men from their labour force, men from both Skye and southern Raasay, to blow up those parts of northern Raasay which Calum required blowing up. The whole exercise cost the Department of Agriculture £1,900. It would prove to be the only outside investment made until Calum MacLeod had completed routing, digging and laying his road.

'When you saw Calum when he was working on the road', said John Nicolson, 'that's all that was on his mind. He would ask your opinion of things, and then he would tell you, "The big rock that's more or less at the fank there at Tarbert – enough gravel there, boy, to cover the road, a bhalaich, from Castle to Fladda."

'That was the type of thing he was seeing. He was foreseeing where he was going to get everything. The boys that used to go over to do the boring and the blasting for him, once every six weeks or so, they were saying to themselves, "Och, that will keep him going for two or three months." But by the time they went back, there was nothing – not a stone was to be seen. It was all in place in the road. You can see his stonework still. It was terrific altogether. It seems practically impossible to do.'

'There were two separate lots of blasting in the first phase,' said Julia MacLeod Allan. 'The first lot of blasting was beyond the south march cattle grid near to Brochel. That had to be blasted out and I remember passing the big compressor blasting that rock. At one blasting where the diversion goes eastwards a hillock was blown up into the air – and it was hollow inside! And there was a pinnacle up at Tarbert, a spear of rock. They used to call it Cailleach an Tairbeart, the Old Woman of Tarbert. It was a tall pinnacle, vaguely reminiscent of that landmark in Skye, the Old Man of Storr. It was just above the road, but later the road had to go through between two rocks and it would be too narrow, so she had to go! That's one bit that I regret, that I don't have a photograph to remind me of that pinnacle.'

When the county men had gone and taken the blasting equipment with them, Calum was once more on his own. 'For years he went off in the morning,' his wife Lexie would say, 'with his piece [lunch] in his bag, and I wouldn't see him again until dark. He was determined to build that road.'

'Oh, there was marvellous talent, you know,' said Jessie Nicolson. "The work he put in there is unbelievable, and with no modern equipment – just the barrow and the pick and the shovel. It was marvellous. And the way he built it up there at Tarbert, his stonework is something to be admired. It's amazing when you take it all in.'

It was all the more amazing and admirable because Calum MacLeod worked throughout his fifties and sixties in some of the most challenging weather conditions in western Europe. It is known that in January 1975, when Calum had almost finished, he experienced the wettest calendar month in Skye and Raasay since 1928, and that fourteen of those thirty-one days were assaulted by winds ranging from strong to gale-force. As for the earlier stages of his labours, it is known that the whole of 1967 was also exceptionally wet, but that by way of compensation the whole of 1968 was exceptionally dry. All of that is known in large part thanks to an acquaintance of Calum MacLeod.

Towards the end of the 1930s Calum first encountered Donald Archie Maclean, then a young man doing brief service as a relief teacher at Torran School. Maclean stood in for Miss Alexandrina Macdonald while the permanent teacher took sick leave in November and December 1938, and while he was in northern Raasay he lodged with the MacLeod family in South Arnish.

D. A. Maclean had been born in 1908 in North Uist in the Outer Hebrides. After qualifying as a teacher he taught for nine years in his home island. During that period, in about 1931, D. A. Maclean first became interested in recording and chronicling the Hebridean weather; 'I started keeping notes,' he would say, 'based on fairly primitive equipment, just an ordinary bottle and filler to measure rainfall.'

It was the beginning of a lifelong preoccupation. After leaving Torran, D. A. Maclean taught at three different schools in Skye. In 1972 he retired to a house in Ellishadder in the parish of Staffin on the north-eastern coast of Skye. There, Donald Archie Maclean improved his equipment and noted and compiled monthly weather reports, which began to appear in the local press as 'Staffin Weather', and would in 1981 be anthologised in booklet form as *Weather in North Skye*, and which won him both local fame and a global network of interested correspondents.

When he was monitoring 'Staffin Weather', Maclean came very close to recording the weather of Arnish in northern Raasay. The two communities are divided by just seven miles of sea. They face each other across the Sound of Raasay. They share far more than divides them: a heritage, a language, a seafaring and fishing tradition, an attachment to the surnames Gillies and MacLeod . . . and the weather. What snow falls on Staffin will almost always fall on Arnish. The storms that blast Ellishadder will progress within minutes to Torran. Their inches of rainfall and hours of sunlight are almost the same. The teacher whose acquaintanceship Calum MacLeod had made in the late 1930s unwittingly devoted much of the rest of his life to a journal of the weather conditions in which Calum worked on his croft, at his postal round, on his lighthouse boat and upon his road.

Calum himself had a kindly view of the microclimate in northern Raasay. Others, lacking his warm familiarity, would be less charitable. The climate of all of Raasay, including the north of Raasay, is characteristically wet and windy – although possibly its chief characteristic is that it has no single characteristic, as the climate of the Hebrides is notoriously variable and unpredictable. In January 1962, 11.41 inches of rain fell on Staffin. And a similar amount fell also upon northern Raasay. But exactly one year later, in January 1963, the local precipitation had fallen by 90 per cent to 1.41 inches. In the whole of the year 1967, while he was laying road foundations somewhere south of the shores of Loch Arnish, a total of over 100 inches of rain was deposited on the head of Calum MacLeod. The average annual rainfall for the United Kingdom is between 20 and 40 inches.

There was never much frost on these shores, where the Gulf Stream breathed its last, and what snow came down did not usually lie for long. But snow certainly did fall, and at curious times of the year. On 9 May 1943 D. A. Maclean noted 4 inches of snow lying in northern Skye, 'with tulips in full bloom and the cuckoo cheerfully (or crazily) singing from the cliffs'.

Winter temperatures were however comparatively mild, and summer temperatures comparatively luke-warm. The average January temperature in central England is roughly 3.8 degrees centigrade. In Skye and Raasay it is 6.5 degrees. The average English July temperature is 16.1 degrees. In Skye and Raasay it is 15.4. The maximum summer temperature over any prolonged period of time on or near the Inner Hebridean seaboard is usually no more than about 21 degrees. In Edinburgh it is 24 degrees, and in Birmingham it is 27 degrees. Skye and Raasay routinely share around 1,200 hours of sunshine a year, compared with Edinburgh's 1,384 and Birmingham's 1,404. Calum MacLeod might not have frozen at his labours, but he was equally unlikely to bake. During May, June and July, the months of longest daylight, the mean daily duration of sunshine is five hours in the islands of northern Scotland, compared to eight hours in the Isle of Wight off the south coast of England. During the months of shortest daylight – November, December and January – there is an average of an hour's sunshine a day in northern Scotland, compared to two hours a day on the south coast of England.

Yet there would be no dependable meteorological routine. During the summer of 1968, while Calum MacLeod was working on the central spine of his road between Brochel and Arnish, the weather beamed upon him. Skye and Raasay enjoyed almost 1,500 hours of sunshine in that climatic *annus mirabilis*, including ten consecutive August days with an average temperature of 19 degrees.

Calum MacLeod would try not to work in the worst of the rain. But one thing would always haunt the man outdoors in Raasay: sheltered in the lee of Skye or not, he could never quite escape the wind. The wind was, and still is, the dominant weather feature. Occasionally, but only occasionally, it took the form of a welcome south-westerly zephyr. More frequently it blew cold breezes into the hottest day. The wind created horizontal hailstorms. The wind drove drizzling rain through the most carefully fitted layers of clothing. The wind alone could make it difficult even for Calum MacLeod to keep his feet.

The United Kingdom is the windiest country in Europe, and the Hebrides are comfortably the windiest part of the UK. A 'day of gale' is defined by the United Kingdom's Meteorological Office as a day on which the mean wind speed at ten metres above ground level reaches thirty-nine miles per hour or more over any period of ten minutes during the twenty-four hours between midnight and midnight. In England the most exposed coasts are those of Devon and Cornwall, where there are about fifteen days of gale a year. Inland, towards Birmingham, London and even Edinburgh, the number of days of gale-force winds decreases to fewer than five a year. The Hebrides experience, on average, about thirty-five days of gale a year. Between 1964 and 1968 Donald Maclean, Calum MacLeod's acquaintance and erstwhile neighbour across the water in Ellishadder, recorded an average of sixty-eight days – or almost 20 per cent of the time – in each passing year when the wind blew between Staffin and northern Raasay at a speed greater than thirty miles per hour.

Yet even the wind would rarely stop Calum working. He worked, as all of his people had always worked, through the worst and the best of weather. He worked hunched up against the storm, bent by the gale, chilled by the cold, sweating in the unaccustomed sun, soaked by unpredicted showers of sleet – sometimes all on the same day. The weather would never

defeat him. The weather would change and go elsewhere. Calum MacLeod would not.

If Calum was indefatigable, the same could not be
said of his tools. He was, on one occasion, levering a
large rock out of the hillside over his road. His
crowbar took purchase of it and the boulder began
to move. It rolled out of the hollow in which it had
stood since the Jurassic Age, tumbled down the slope,
struck the road, bounced once and landed on top of
his wheelbarrow, spatchcocking it to the ground. In
total Calum worked his way through three wheel-
barrows, six picks, six shovels, five sledgehammers,
four spades and one crowbar while building the road
between Brochel Castle and Arnish. It was estimated
that the largest single boulder he removed weighed
nine tons. It stood in the path of his road. He used a
jack to lift it, then packed it in place with stones, then
jacked it up again, then repacked it with stones,
then jacked it once more . . . until it had been heaved
out of his way and had fallen, defeated, into the sea.
He was accompanied on his painstaking travail between Brochel Castle and Arnish by a tiny portable
storage hut which edged its way, yard by yard,
month by month, year by year, along the verge in
line with Calum's progress.

Having animals to milk and feed, and other crofting chores to complete, Calum MacLeod could not
spend all of every working day on the road. His early
attempts to keep track of the hours through modern
timekeeping devices failed, as one wrist- or pocket-

watch after another was smashed during his heavy manual labour. So he resorted to a basic portable sundial. This was no more than a stick put upright into the ground. 'It was surprisingly accurate', said his daughter. 'He would return home with a half-hour margin of error. And it fascinated his grand-children!'

Calum MacLeod's hours were restricted not only by his lighthouse shifts and his crofting work, but also by the fact that he was a deeply religious man. Like most other Raasay people, he was a member of the Free Presbyterian Church of Scotland and a committed Sabbatarian. He observed family worship twice a day, and any house guests or visitors were expected to participate. He was precentor, leading the singing of Gaelic psalmody, at the church services held in Fladda School. He would do nothing but essential or humanitarian work between midnight on Saturday and midnight on Sunday, and his road could in the strictest sense be described neither as essential nor as humanitarian. 'Of course the Sab-bath was sacrosanct', said his daughter. 'And I think that did help, because my father worked very hard for six days, and on the other day he would deal with the animals, see that the cows, the dog, and the cats were fed and watered and whatever – and then, if he was not attending church services, it was his day. He would read a bit, or lie on the bed and read some more, and he usually had a snooze in the afternoon. There was this unwinding and recharging of batteries, and I felt that really kept things going. He didn't burn out.'

His faith revived him. It gave him strength and fortitude. It also informed the way that Calum Mac-Leod viewed the world outside Arnish. He personally lived a long way from the 'permissive society' of the 1960s and early '70s, but he was made aware of it, and had come to perceive the moral decline of British society as interconnected with six years of socialist government, centralisation, and the apparently wilful persecution of such communities as northern Raasay. In September 1970 a typically idiosyncratic volume of reading material caused him to write another letter to the *Stornoway Gazette*.

'Before me', he wrote in his careful, cursive, educated hand, 'lies the "History of Ancient Egypt", published 1809. Formerly described as the "granary of the Ancient World" and "the cradle of arts and sciences", Egypt was "flourishing, polite and learned, whilst Europe was immersed in grossest ignorance and barbarism. Once the most learned and flourishing society on earth, yet Egypt was reduced to the lowest state of degradation where the usual bonds of society seem as if eternally separated" . . .

'There is reference to allegations of transactions with crocodiles. I fully believe that were these reptiles common to our riverbanks, Socialists in their apathy to crime or evils would not ban this abomination, but would gladly seize the opportunity to licence and tax as harmless amusement . . . were the Socialists conforming to the law of God when they passed the Abortion, Capital Punishment and Homosexual Bills?'*

Calum MacLeod was the very definition of an

* As this letter attracted a bewildered response from other readers of the *Gazette*, who were especially startled by Calum's reference to 'transactions with crocodiles', it probably requires explanation. The other correspondents may not have known that Calum MacLeod was repeating a common nineteenth-century misunderstanding. It seems likely that Calum was reading an English translation of *Description de l'Égypte*, a comprehensive study of the country made by French scholars who had travelled there with Napoleon's conquering army in 1798, which was published in a number of volumes between 1809 and 1828. This flawed but original work was extremely influential. Its assertion that Egyptian fellahin had congress with crocodiles as part of divine worship was picked up lasciviously by the English explorer and author Sir Richard Burton, who quoted a French traveller's account of bestiality he witnessed among the fellahin of Egypt. The men, taking advantage of the female crocodile's helpless position, drive off the male and 'supplant him in this frightful intercourse'. This congress, adds Burton, is believed to be 'the sovereignest, for rising to rank and riches'.

The truth appears to have been comparatively mundane. The Egyptian fellahin did indeed worship crocodiles. But in order to worship them suitably, they needed to know their gender. As a crocodile's gender is not superficially apparent this was and is notoriously difficult, requiring delicate manual exploration of the reptile. 'To be certain of a crocodilian's sex', writes a modern veterinarian, 'you need to either feel or visually identify the penis (male) or clitoris (female). In big animals, this is very easy . . . In smaller animals, however, it requires a lot more experience and skill to do it properly and not make a mistake . . . Although this procedure does not harm the animal if performed correctly, crocodilians generally object to such demeaning behaviour. Therefore, the animal should be restrained by a second person throughout the procedure.'

It would seem that the influential French travellers had observed Egyptians sexing crocodiles, or seen or heard descriptions of the same, and had jumped to the wrong conclusion.

autodidact, a self-taught polymath. He learned both academically, from reading often arcane volumes, and empirically, from a life spent outside at sea and on dry land. By the end of the 1960s there was clearly nobody else available who knew more about the past and present, the botany and geology of northern Raasay. When such an august body as the Botanical Society of the British Isles (BSBI) held a field meeting in Raasay in 1969 he was their obvious point of contact, and he did not disappoint them. 'Arnish and Torran', read the *BSBI Journal* report in the following year, 'turned out to contain more woodland than anywhere apart from Raasay House – mainly birch and hazel, with *Hymenophyllum wilsonii* on the mossy boulders. With the assistance of Mr Malcolm MacLeod we located *Lythrum salicaria* – difficult to find when only 4 in. high!'

'Oh, plantlife!' Calum would say to Derek Cooper four years later. 'Well, there's even wild strawberries. I was with botanists, and we found 531 different species in the area, of plants. Some were known in Britain. In fact we got one or two, and they said that they could be only found in the limestone rocks in Kent.'*

---

* The local botanist Stephen Bungard commented on the subject, 'There are about that many [531] types of plant on Raasay as long as one counts planted species and microspecies. There is nothing here not known elsewhere in Britain. Raasay limestone has some plants in common with the limestone in Kent, and more or less everywhere else in the UK. Calum showed the BSBI purple loosestrife near Torran – not easy to spot as it never flowered while the sheep were there.'

There would come a time when not only botanists but also journalists, radio presenters and television crews made the pilgrimage to Calum MacLeod's front door. But Derek Cooper was the first to recognise that something extraordinary was happening in the north end of Raasay. An energetic and productive broadcaster and writer, Cooper's maternal family came from Skye and Lewis. He had spent school holidays in Portree and had ever since been in thrall to the Hebrides.

Cooper walked up to Arnish in 1972 and tape-recorded an interview with Calum for the BBC Radio Four programme *It Takes All Sorts*. 'The voice of a fully authentic crofter,' reported the *Daily Telegraph* at the end of May, 'one of the few still living on the Hebridean island of Raasay, was heard in conversation with Derek Cooper in *It Takes All Sorts* on Thursday.

'Calum MacLeod cheerfully makes a living there and is building a road to his land single-handed. Aged 58 or so, he had "never been in the hands of a doctor, a dentist or a nurse". He told Mr Cooper: "It's a fine, healthy life here. No dirty air and no chance of being run down by a car."

'He was a great find for radio: a farmer of high intelligence and with a gift of self-expression in English far from difficult to Sassenach ears; it was not surprising to learn that this refreshingly unambitious man had turned in at least one prize-winning essay.'

Derek Cooper returned to Arnish on a wet summer's

day in 1973 with a BBC television film crew to make a thirty-minute documentary entitled *The Island That Nearly Made It* for the BBC's 'Breathing Space' slot. Cooper followed the current postman, John Ferguson, from the south end of the island to Brochel, where Ferguson prudently parked the red post office Morris Minor van and walked up the rough surface of Calum's highway.

'A few months ago', Cooper commented in a voice as gravelly as the road, 'this [telegraph] line came down in a gale. The only link with Arnish in the north. Calum MacLeod, who lives there, was cut off. Well, nothing new in that. He's been cut off all his life. The public road ends at Brochel Castle. Boswell and Johnson walked up here 200 years ago, following this same trek. From now on [Brochel] you have to go by foot.

'For generations the people who lived up in Arnish carried everything in and out on their backs. And you still do it today. Fifty years ago the hundred or so people living in the north of Raasay petitioned the county council for a road. But there never seemed to be any money available, the plan was always being shelved. It was not a request that had much priority . . . And so the people began to leave. The school was closed; the telephone kiosk removed; Arnish died.

'But one man is thinking of tomorrow. Four years ago, armed with little more than a wheelbarrow, a pickaxe and a spade, Calum MacLeod began to convert this track into a road. His neighbour gave him a hand. The Department of Agriculture, who own Raa-

say, sent some men to help him blast past the worst
bits. But virtually the whole of this 6,000 feet of road is
built by the sweat of his brow. Now it's nearly finished, they say he ought to get a medal. They're saying
on the island that this homemade highway to Arnish
has a better foundation than any other road. Calum's
embankments are built with great skill. You can see
that here there's a craftsman's hand at work.'

Derek Cooper's commentary ran on top of a short
colour film of Calum working on the road beyond
Tarbert, within sight of Loch Arnish and the far shores
of Torran. He is wearing denim jeans and – unusually,
for he would normally work in leather footwear –
Wellington boots, a navy blue jacket and a Guernsey,
and beneath his lighthouse-keeper's cap his cropped
hair is white. Calum first comes into camera-shot
pushing his wheelbarrow southwards from Arnish.
Inside the barrow are a shovel, a sledgehammer and
a pickaxe. He takes off his jacket and drops it on the
ground. He picks up the shovel and with it tears a
lump of heather and sod from the cliff-face. It is an
extremely large piece of earth and vegetation. As he
drags it with his pickaxe down from the cliff to the
road and drops it ruthlessly over the seaward side, we
see that this thick lump of heather and sod is almost
the same size and weight as Calum himself. He moves
it not without effort, but with a determination that will
brook no resistance. The camera lingers on the astonishing dry-stone works that support the flat, dry road.

Calum then attacks the cliff-face with his pickaxe

and brings down a shower of rocks. He sorts through the stones with his bare hands, throwing useless scraps of vegetation over his shoulder and down towards the sea. He picks up four very large chunks of granite and puts them inside the worn, wooden wheelbarrow, which was clearly homemade and is attached to a cast-iron frame and wheel.

As the camera pans back, the television screen again displays the magnitude and jigsaw-like precision of Calum's finished holding wall on the seaward side of the road. He wheels the four large rocks a few yards further towards Arnish before tipping them out of the barrow. Then he begins to slot them into place on the landward side of the road. He stoops and handles the heavy stones with the agility and strength of a gymnast or a coalminer. He stops to wrench off his right boot and tip a stray pebble from its depths.

'Alongside the stone dykes built by his father and grandfather', explains Cooper, 'are the new culverts of Calum's motor road to Arnish. All this has been done in between working his croft single-handed and serving as a relief lighthouse keeper on Rona. Sixty now, Calum has the energy and determination of a man half his age. When he was younger he won a gold medal for one of his Gaelic essays. He has a feeling for the world about him, for the sea, and the land, and the ancient rocks beneath his feet.'

Calum MacLeod's assured, gentle voice then overtakes that of Derek Cooper. 'The rocks here', he says, 'are very interesting indeed. Geologically, it's a geologist's paradise. You won't go a couple of yards when you see different types of rock. Mica, quartz, felspar, fossils and whatnot. And even copper seams have been discovered here.'

Calum is next seen facing the camera in close-up, with the sea of Loch Arnish and a single house at Torran visible over his right shoulder. He is still wearing his old lighthouse cap. He has a steady, patient expression. He is listening carefully to the question. 'It's ironic in a way, isn't it,' says Cooper, 'that you're building this road right at the end of the life of the community, because virtually everyone has gone from this north end, from Arnish, except yourself?'

'Yes,' replies Calum quickly, 'but nobody here had a freehold like me. All the rest, their houses were built at the landlord's expense. And any improvements they did was simply a compensation on you leaving, depending on the state of your house. If your house was in a poor condition you wouldn't get a penny.'

'How long do you think it's going to be before you at last run the Land Rover along the road to your croft?'

Calum looks sharply, seriously to his right, indicating with his lean face the close proximity of Torran and Arnish. 'About three months. And I'll get it right through to my croft. Once I get the road joined here, you see, it'll be fit for my Land Rover to go through. So I'm within 400 yards of my house already, and once this diversion is joined up and cleared, the rest is plain sailing.'

'Will there be a ceremony when you ride along it?'

Calum smiles softly, almost imperceptibly, with his eyes rather than his mouth, for this is a harmless question. 'Oh well, very likely,' he says. 'I'll be running back and fore with the Land Rover the first couple of days, non-stop.' Then his features relax and he chuckles slowly, not to the camera and not to Derek Cooper, but to himself.

'The road itself is a major triumph,' Cooper would write later in *Hebridean Connection*. 'Calum has built culverts, blasted rockfaces, dug hillsides away almost in a spirit of desperation. No agency outside the island was going to do it, therefore he must hew it himself.

' "We petitioned the County Council to build a road years ago," [said Calum]. "It was put off and off and the people went one by one . . . When they saw what I was doing the Department [of Agriculture] kindly offered to do the blasting and the [Skye] District Council have been very helpful too."

'Calum built his road in what spare time he had left after working his croft and keeping watch at the lighthouse on Rona as a relief keeper. Last year he took 1,000 stooks of oats off his five acres, sufficient to keep seven cows, a calf and two stirks . . .

'Calum looks with pride along the empty length of his road winding round Loch Arnish, not metalled yet, but almost ready for a Land Rover . . . "I always like freedom," [said Calum]. "It's a fine healthy life on the hills here. I have never been an hour off duty by illness, or ever in the hands of a doctor or dentist or nurse or anybody in my life and that's the truth."

'John [Ferguson] and I walk back to Brochel where we left the van. "They say that Calum's road is better bottomed than any other road on Raasay," says John. "It's a pity it wasn't built thirty years ago, maybe there'd be more people living up there now."'

As he worked, Calum MacLeod dug into his people's deepest past. On one occasion, towards the end of his journey, as he approached his own croft, he turned up a perfectly formed and preserved Neolithic axe-head. 'I was digging out a soft patch and replacing it with stone,' he would tell the writer Ian Grimble in 1984. 'And I was down about 18 inches or thereabouts, getting close to the rock. This [axe-head] came up. And I looked at it and I remembered then what I saw in a book . . . So I came home with this stone and compared it with what was in the book.' It was a greenstone axe-head, still with a functional cutting edge. 'I have handled millions of pieces of stone in my time,' said Calum, 'and I have never seen anything like this – It is not Raasay stone by any means. I believe it to have been made in the Lake District in Stone Age times, although how it got to Raasay, I don't know – although they have also been found in Denmark.'

That ancient implement appeared almost as a confirmation, as evidence that people had been living and working and practising stonework in Arnish for millennia. (They had also, it might be added, been trading with and travelling to and from other distant regions of Neolithic Europe. Use of the open seaways was no recent phenomenon.) It measured roughly four inches by two, fitting snugly into the palm of Calum MacLeod's hand. It was sent to Edinburgh for archaeological assessment, but there was not really any need. Calum understood it perfectly.

He understood also the significance of the stretch of road that he built two thirds of the way between Brochel and Arnish, where the narrowest ridge of northern Raasay came down to Loch Arnish. George Rainy's deer wall still stood there, apparently immutable, as big and as brash and as apparently unbreachable as ever, 100 years after it had been erected to define the difference in value between people and imported sheep or game.

Calum MacLeod pushed his road through George Rainy's wall; snapped the deer fence off where it reached down to the sea and left its western edge crumbling into the hillside. There is, of course, no recorded date for this symbolic event. It probably took place in stages in the very early months of the 1970s. But significant clues lie round about. Directly below the suddenly abridged end of the wall lies the sheep fold – or fank – of the MacLeod family of Arnish. A northbound traveller along Calum's road would pass the end of the wall on their right and the sheep fank on their left. The wall, even broken and pointless, would still be impressive, snaking up its shallow glen and dipping beyond sight over the hill, towards the eastern sea.

But the sheep fank below was and would remain a miniature Machu Picchu of stonecraft by comparison; a bewildering maze of worked granite, created and extended and embellished by succeeding generations of the masons of Arnish. Stone fank complexes are not unique to the Hebrides, but stone fank complexes which cause the traveller to pause and smile are rare. It has a practical logic of its own. Those small entrances with perfect lintels are there to admit and release sheep; not to conjure images of ancient human habitation. Those horseshoe walls dissolve into and out of the granite of the hillside because it is sensible for them to follow that course; not in order to suggest a native affinity with the environment.

Above the fank and below the end of George Rainy's wall the road ran past in a graceful arc. In this immediate area, as elsewhere, Calum MacLeod had built perfect holding walls. He had trimmed the cliffside edge of the road with boulders, to prevent any careless motorist from driving into the sea. Where the burn ran down beside the wall he built a culvert to allow the fresh running water free passage to Loch Arnish. He laid faggots of birchwood on the ground to cushion the flagstones which would form the base of the culvert. Then he built the small culvert walls. Then he built the road on top of that, burying his creation, hiding it from sight.

All of that was purely practical. Any other interpretation is imaginative. But, as Calum's friend and former neighbour Donald MacLeod would muse, 'Not far south of Arnish he broke down the wall with which George Rainy had enclosed his sheep-tack . . . I imagine a big cheer went up in his heart when he did that.'

In some of the latter stages he had another form of help. Calum and Lexie MacLeod briefly gained some new neighbours when Raasay's retired district nurse Nancy Park and her husband John moved into the Arnish croft tenancy and the house which had been vacated by Calum's sister, brother and mother. John Park had the welcome asset of a tractor and was happy to assist – the Parks were attracted to Arnish as much by the prospect of a decent access road as by the calm and beauty of the place. Nonetheless, Calum's road would not be finished, as he had hoped, by the end of 1973, just as it had not been finished, as he had predicted to Basil Reckitt eight years earlier, in 1970. The date of its completion is as obscure as the year of its commencement, and for even better reasons. When is a road finished? Is a road ever finished? He was certainly able by 1974 to drive his Land Rover or any tractor in the ample if uneven space between his exquisite stonework from Arnish to Brochel and back again. But no doctor's or nurse's car, no ambulance, no post office van and few civilian vehicles would last the course of such a two-mile road until it had been properly metalled, surfaced and tarmacked.

He wanted it finished and then properly maintained to County Council roads department standards. Of that there will be no doubt. But even unfinished he considered it functional. Calum MacLeod would not bow to the minor practical limitations of what he had created. He insisted upon driving the Land Rover which he had bought – in careful anticipation of completion in the early 1970s – up and down the stone road. 'The first time he drove it', said his daughter, 'he was amazed at how fast the bracken moved towards him! But he never went any further than the end of the road.'

That was because, just as Calum had grown tobacco although he did not smoke, and as he cultivated tomatoes without ever eating them, so Calum Mac-Leod, who would shortly become the most celebrated amateur road builder in twentieth-century Scotland, had never taken and would never pass his driving test.

A Kind of
Historical Justification

It'll be like an autobahn.

Calum MacLeod, October 1982

The fact that the new road between Brochel Castle and Arnish was increasingly noted and recognised as a wonder of the modern world did not make its passage – in any literal or metaphorical sense of the word, by car or through a maze of bureaucracies – especially easy, as the visiting exiles were the first to discover.

'My husband and I', said Jessie Nicolson, 'went there with the car before the road was finished. I was never so scared in all my life – going over boulders – I was holding on! I'll never forget that. It was frightening. It was frightening at the best of times.'

By 1974 Calum MacLeod had completed, or almost completed, just short of two miles of miraculous landscape sculpture. Many rural roads qualify for that compound noun. Calum's road attracted the adjective because he had created it alone. In some eyes his 'land art' was then at its idealised best. The stonework was stunningly complete. The concept was pure and the execution was unsullied. It was by no means kind to any ordinary motorist's suspension or nerves. It was not yet complete, not yet entirely 'practical for vehicular travel', as the art student Campbell Sandilands would later acknowledge, but it had an incomparable artistic 'majesty and splendour'.

'I remember the first time I drove along that road,' said John Nicolson. 'We only reached where the deer fence is. I couldn't get up that brae at the Arnish side. That would have been in a Morris Minor in the mid 1970s. But the road wasn't metalled then. My wife and I were going to stay in Torran for the night, and we set off to take the car as far as it would take us. We parked it just before you come in sight of the deer fence at the corner there, and we walked from there to Torran. Which I thought was a terrific achievement!'

'Calum's road as it stands now (or rather as it runs and teeters and skitters and lurches now)', Magnus Magnusson would suggest of that unfinished article, 'is a work of art in itself, a monument worth preserving in its original form.'

Calum MacLeod certainly did have a vision, and it deserved artistic recognition. It was the vision articulated at the end of Campbell Sandilands' dissertation: 'It will open up ground suitable to young crofters,' Calum said of his work of 'land art'. 'I hope I will live to see people moving back to this lovely area.' So Magnus Magnusson was mistaken to suggest that 'I don't think a bureaucratic resurfacing of [the road] will make much difference to Calum now.' It would make a world of difference.

If Calum's road was to be art, it must be utilitarian art. All the dry-stone dykes, culverts and holding walls would ultimately be worthless if nobody could or would drive along the road they supported. They were not there purely to be looked at and admired. They were there to admit motorised transport to the north end of Raasay. In order for this to happen the road must be finished by heavy machinery and given a smooth topping of tarmacadam. That process would be considered by Calum MacLeod not as a dilution of his achievement but as its completion – as its final, unanswerable statement. It would also constitute a belated but satisfactory admission by local government in Inverness and Portree of their own earlier shortcomings. If then the road still qualified as art, it would be the art of Sydney Harbour Bridge or the Hoover Dam, which were dependent upon their function. If then it failed to qualify as art, it would still do service as a country road.

It would take almost another decade for that vision to be realised. There were false starts and dashed hopes along the way. The first came from the European Economic Community (EEC). The United Kingdom had joined the EEC on the first day of January 1973. Almost immediately Inverness County Council cooked up a scheme designed to persuade the EEC to part-subsidise a £220,000 development of the road from

Brochel Castle as far as Fladda, covering both of Calum's two roads.*

The EEC scheme fell into the mire of local and county politics. Its essential composition required the British government to stump up half of the money, or £110,000, Inverness County Council to fork out another quarter, or £55,000, while the EEC weighed in with the last £55,000. This substantial sum of British taxpayers' and local ratepayers' money was unacceptable to many people, including the Raasay representative on Skye District Council, Alistair Nicolson. 'I would not have any objection to the expenditure by Inverness CC or the EEC of a few thousand pounds to surface the road Malcolm MacLeod has made', wrote councillor Nicolson at the time. But he questioned 'the sense' of spending £220,000 to build a road to a place whose 'population of two cannot by any stretch of the imagination be described as a community. Is it honest for the council to put their hands in our pockets and take all this money so as to qualify for £55,000 from the EEC . . . ?'

That proposal sank out of sight, and was pursued by another. In August 1975 the *West Highland Free Press* reported that 'The truly astonishing story of Calum MacLeod's road on Raasay is about to reach its

---

* If this scheme had gone ahead, Calum himself could not have missed the irony. Its chief sponsor was the county council which he had accused in print of 'neglect and maladministration'. Its chief facilitator would have been the EEC, which he would later accuse of 'chaos and malpractice'.

conclusion. Within the next couple of weeks a team of Royal Engineers will move onto the island to surface the two and a quarter miles of road [*sic*] that the man built with a pick, a wheelbarrow and his bare hands.'

The scheme actually involved 518 Company of the Royal Pioneer Corps and was the brainchild of the Highlands and Islands Development Board. One week after its initial report the *West Highland Free Press* was obliged to note that 'our story . . . was quickly overtaken by events . . . the Highlands and Islands Development Board, who are acting as go-betweens, have now heard that due to "operational priorities" [the Royal Pioneer Corps] are unable to undertake the work for the time being. But, said a Board spokesman, "they're still very keen on it – it's just a matter of getting the time."'

They never did get the time. Dark and unevidenced rumours circulated once more about the malicious intervention of one or another of the Inverness-shire landowner-councillors, and the Royal Pioneer Corps stayed away from northern Raasay.

In 1975 Inverness County Council was abolished and Calum MacLeod found himself paying rates to a new local authority. Its name was the Highland Regional Council. It was based in the same administrative headquarters in Inverness, it retained most of the old officials and it was comprised of many of the old councillors. But it no longer had responsibility for the Outer Isles between Harris and Vatersay, which had been subsumed into a new Western Isles Islands' authority. The few islands still governed from Inverness included Skye, however, and Skye's satellite neighbours of Raasay, Fladda, Rona and Tighe.

If there was no dramatic change in personnel, there was a marginal shift of perspective. Inverness County Council had lost Harris, the Uists, Barra and Vatersay amid charges of neglect. Highland Regional Council was consequently sensitive to such allegations from its remaining island dependants. At the very least, one or two councillors and one or two officials considered themselves mandated to take a fresh look at the requirements of their insular peripheries.

In these new circumstances, in August 1977 a memo was sent from Inverness to the regional council's subdivisional engineer in Portree, asking him to cast light on a certain homemade road between Brochel Castle and Arnish in the north of Raasay. Three weeks later, following a trip to Raasay, the engineer replied to his director of roads and transport.

'This is the road that gained considerable publicity a few years ago', wrote the engineer from Skye, 'as it was constructed over a number of years by a sole crofter.

'. . . it can only be traversed with a Land Rover and is generally extremely rough, with steep hills and many bad bends. The existing surface is generally very loose and rough . . . The road is, of course, unadopted.

'To bring this road up to a standard suitable for adoption, you would be talking in a price of well over £100,000 [over £420,000 today], but if a job creation project was considered any price between £10,000 and

£15,000 could be put on the scheme, but to substantially improve this track a high proportion would be required in machine and machine time and cost of materials.' At least it could be said that, after half a century and the loss of 98 per cent of the population of northern Raasay, Inverness was looking seriously at the road between Brochel and Arnish. A key to the reason may be found in the observation of the Skye divisional engineer that 'This is the road that gained considerable publicity a few years ago, as it was constructed over a number of years by a sole crofter.'

Calum MacLeod was, as Derek Cooper, Radio Four and the *Daily Telegraph* had revealed, and a score of later journalists and broadcasters would discover, excellent copy. His road was an irrefutable achievement. But if the man behind it had been slightly less intriguing, less charming, less perfectly rounded in his presentation of the independent but beleaguered Gaelic crofter resisting with infinite wile and resourcefulness the baleful forces of government, it might never have gained quite so much publicity.

That is not to say that Calum MacLeod presented an artificial front. He did not, because he did not need to. He was fully aware of the power of his case and the seductive charms of his culture and way of life. He simply needed no persuasion to advertise them. And if the broadcast result was a little more Brigadoon than he, more than anybody, knew the reality to be, he could shrug and chuckle.

Calum would become a celebrated subject for celebrity journalists, and it cannot have been a comfortable experience for councillors and council officials, past and present. Magnus Magnusson, the Icelander who had become a popular television quizmaster, would turn up to discover that Calum's road 'is officially designated as a "public footpath", but in fact it takes tractors or 4-wheel drive vehicles at a leisurely pace – about 4 mph, ideally, making a journey of about half an hour. The surface leaves something to be desired; but the bottoming – ah, that is something that road-men will sing about for years to come!

'Calum is retired from the Lighthouse Service now. He and his wife live in a little red-roofed crofthouse with whitewashed walls (fully modernised by Calum himself, of course) in the marvellously sheltered and fertile dell of South Arnish. Here, by the sweat of his brow, Calum MacLeod has created a veritable Shangri-La. His house is crammed with books, for winter reading and study. He and his wife have milk from their own cow, they grow their own vegetables, their larder overflows with fish and rabbit-meat (he's a dab hand at the sea-fishing and with a gun); and he is also an accomplished knitter – he has two Knitmasters . . .

'People might say that Calum MacLeod is eccentric. I suppose he is, in the dictionary sense that "he differs from the usual in behaviour". Last year, for instance, he added another acre to his eight acres of arable land by reclaiming an area of boggy, rush-ridden rough grazing. The ground was too uneven for a tractor, so Calum tackled it with a spade and the traditional

Hebridean foot-plough, the cas-chrom. Eccentric? Perhaps – but you should have seen his first crop of oats.

'Calum is a living reminder to us all of what the peasant crofting culture of the Gaels is capable of producing, if we ever need reminding: the lad o' pairts who becomes the man for all seasons. A lot of people write knowingly about crofting and its cultures; Calum not only writes about it – he lives it.'

That kind of coverage, and there was and would be a good deal more of it, made difficult reading in the government offices of Edinburgh, Inverness and even Portree. Magnusson might reach the personal conclusion that for artistic reasons Calum's road should not receive a 'bureaucratic resurfacing', but the broadcaster stressed that that was his own aesthetic preference, and did not diminish the legitimacy of Calum's claim. 'Certainly,' wrote Magnusson, 'Calum MacLeod and his neighbour in South Arnish deserve a decent road to help them maximise their efforts as crofters. Certainly, a proper road north of Brochel Castle might encourage a repopulation of the north of Raasay. Certainly, a road to Arnish, 55 years after that first petition by the islanders, would have a kind of historical justification about it.'

In such very public circumstances Highland Regional Council had no serious option but to act, or at least to try to act. Sam MacNaughton, a future head of county transport services, would recall, 'When Calum's road was being built I was in contract administration in Inverness, controlling the budgets and sucking in monies through grants and other avenues as contributions towards our projects. I was involved in Calum's road since we managed to get a township road grant from the Scottish Development Department towards the cost.'

There were a dozen different avenues through which finance and manpower could be attracted to Calum MacLeod's road from a dozen different bodies. At least two of them – the EEC and the British military – had previously been attempted and had failed. The question facing Sam MacNaughton and his colleagues at the end of the 1970s was which one next, and at what cost: £10,000, £15,000, £100,000 or more? According to the divisional engineer in Portree in November 1978, 'the Brochel–Arnish Road would cost approx £50,000 to be improved under this system [the Scottish Development Department's Township Roads grant scheme], at a cost per head of the resident population of £12,500, and at this cost the scheme would be unlikely to receive approval from the Scottish Development Department.' The Skye divisional engineer then suggested that as the Township Roads scheme was unlikely to come through, his own Unadopted Roads Budget could foot the bill – if it received a 100 per cent budget increase!

At sixty-seven years of age, Calum himself was impressed by neither the idea of a four-year Township Roads scheme nor the different council engineers' 'fantastic estimation' of the cost. 'I have lived to see vehicles', he wrote to the roads department of Highland Regional Council in August 1978, 'from the JCB to "Beatles" [Volkswagen Beetles] using the road at the total cost [of] £1190 to the DOAFS [Department of Agriculture and Fisheries Scotland] who helped me [the actual cost had been £1,900], but not one penny from your Department or Council while I paid the full Road Tax for my vehicles – and that for over ten years – this in addition to that paid by other users.

'To delay improvement for a further four years is simply following the infamous tactics of infamous maladministration pursued by your ignominious predecessors for over fifty-four years, with disastrous consequences to this area.'

In the council offices of Portree and Inverness, at the headquarters of the Highlands and Islands Development Board, in the Scottish Development Department in Edinburgh, at Department of Agriculture suboffices the length of Scotland, Calum's road was threatening to cause chronic migraine.

Early in 1979 another divisional engineer visited the road. Upon his return to Skye from Raasay he scribbled his impressions in pencil upon a sheet of paper. 'The existing road has been constructed', he wrote, 'over the past 10 years by Mr Callum MacLeod No 1 & 2 South Arnish assisted by Mr Parks No 3 & 4 periodically. The road has been constructed from a plan proposed by an engineer from the Royal Engineers some time ago. Mr MacLeod had the assistance of the Dept of Ag and Fisheries in the form of labour and machinery where blasting was required.

'Otherwise, he has constructed the road himself, building drystone retaining walls where the road is in need of embankment and forming a roadbase of rock and gravel from the borders along the length of the road. The horizontal and vertical alignment of the road, considering the location and volume of traffic, are adequate and basically what is required to bring the road to adoptable standards is a small amount of rock excavation to widen the road at various points, some drain work, 4″ of bottoming throughout, basically to regulate the surface and bitmac* surface.'

It is difficult not to discern here a discrepancy in approach, even a clash of attitudes. However essentially practical he may have been, Calum MacLeod carried the weight of his people's history on his shoulders and in his mind. Council bureaucrats and engineers, however imaginative and however willing to be sympathetic, saw nothing but a bumpy, dusty track to nowhere. Calum saw children playing and old ladies enjoying the autumn of their lives in Arnish, Umachan, Torran and Fladda. Officials saw ruined houses, no electricity, overgrown crofts, and a lost community which no highway on earth could restore. They could rarely have understood the debt of gratitude which Calum MacLeod felt to the place which had raised him and his family in health, the place which had provided him with everything that he

---

* 'Bitmac' is the proper, road engineers' name for tarmac. Tarmacadam is technically known as 'bituminous macadam', or 'bitmac' for short.

held dear. Calum knew what Hebridean ghost towns looked like; he walked through them every week. He was determined that his beloved South Arnish would not share the fate of Umachan and Kyle Rona.

But it was this unexceptional report, fine-tuned and typed up, which apparently persuaded the Scottish Development Department to acknowledge on 13 February 1979 that the proposal to upgrade and improve Calum MacLeod's road from Brochel to Arnish through a Township Road Grant 'does seem to be eligible'. The cost, Highland Council estimated, would be £45,000 (£150,000 today). 'We would expect the SDD', a council official told the press, 'to make a decision on whether or not to provide a grant within six months. Only if they do provide a grant will we act.'

Six months passed and no decision was forthcoming. Eight months passed, and in September the council's divisional engineer, Michael Courtney, informed the Department of Agriculture's estate office in Portree in writing that 'The Brochel/South Arnish route is currently being submitted by the Regional Council to the Scottish Development Department for grant assistance under the Township Road Programme and the Congested Districts Act, but I have no indication to hand how this application is being considered.'

Early in 1980 the MP for Inverness-shire, Russell Johnston, was made aware that a year had passed since the Scottish Development Department's acknowledgement of Calum's road's 'eligibility', but that nothing had since happened. Russell Johnston elicited a reply from an under-secretary of state at the Scottish Office, Malcolm Rifkind MP, which assured him that 'This application is being given urgent consideration, and it is hoped to issue a decision soon.'

In fact, Calum's road had become a victim of the local authority spending cuts which were immediately enforced by Margaret Thatcher's and Malcolm Rifkind's Conservative government following its election in May 1979. Highland Regional Council did not finally deliver to the Scottish Development Department all of the required details of the project until June 1979, a month after that election. Once the scale of the public spending cuts were made clear, it became apparent to the council that – whatever the Scottish Development Department decided – they themselves would not be able to fill their own side of the bargain in that financial year. 'There was no point', said Philip Shimmin, Highland Regional Council's depute director of roads and transport, 'in applying for something in 1979 that we couldn't afford to start that year.'

So the application to the Scottish Development Department, carried forward by twelve months and with a revised estimated cost of £80,000 (£230,000 today) was posted from Inverness to Edinburgh in February 1980. It was approved. In November 1980 Calum MacLeod's landlords, the Department of Agriculture and Fisheries, formally gave Highland Regional Council permission to cross the common grazings in northern Raasay 'for the purpose of carrying out improvements to the Brochel–South Arnish township road'. Four conditions were attached to this permission. The last one stated that 'The Highland Regional Council shall maintain the said road in the condition in which it is, consequential upon the completion of the work to be carried out.'

On paper at least, Calum MacLeod had won his long war. The former enemy had committed itself to reparation. Calum was a Christian, and was not given to gloating. But he was also a Celt, and was inclined to rhapsody. He would write a ballad to recall the concept, immortalise the toil and celebrate the imminent final stages of his highway.

> Yet I was undismayed, [it read in part]
> With peg and line and level too
> its course was then surveyed.
> No bulldozer was to be got,
> no crusher and no digger
> Just brawn and strength to do the lot,
> and, working like a nigger.
> For six long years the work goes on
> by crags or mossy hollows.
> The tourists are amazed to find
> a road they now can follow
> Round many a curve and rocky cliff
> the road now does meander,
> and you will find a motor-car
> where only sheep could wander.
> And, when at last it is complete,

the battle will be over,
and walking will be obsolete
We all go by Landrover.
The road a monument will remain
in memory of one fellow
who saw his countrymen swept away
by the heirs of Patrick Sellar.

The war of words had indeed been won. But on stone and earth and bitmac there were still skirmishes to fight. As Calum MacLeod passed his seventieth birthday in 1981 the council's six-man Raasay road squad had still been unable to start work on his road. The further delay was due to the fact that, for a variety of reasons, £80,000 would no longer cover the bill. Thanks to inflation, £80,000 in the summer of 1982 was worth rather less than £80,000 in February of 1980. And neither Calum nor his road were getting any younger . . .

'As a result of adverse weather,' Highland Council's capital works depute director Sam MacNaughton wrote to the Scottish Development Department in November 1981, 'and in particular the exceptional rainfall over the period since 1979, large areas of the existing track are now severely damaged and a recent estimate based on an updated survey of the track's condition has indicated that the present estimated cost for the work is likely to be approximately £120,000 compared with the original estimate of £80,000. On these considerations I would like to resubmit this scheme for grant on the basis of the revised cost.'

The Scottish Development Department replied to MacNaughton requesting further details of and justification for the increased grant to finish Calum's road. Sam MacNaughton's reply illustrated a sea change in Invernesian attitudes towards what had previously been their headache in South Arnish.

'The two inhabited crofts in South Arnish', wrote MacNaughton, 'are vigorously worked with the remaining uninhabited crofts and common grazings well stocked. The provision of a proper access will permit the bulk deliveries of foodstuffs and fertiliser for reseeding and reclamation purposes. The improved access will make the crofts easier to work and make the area more attractive to live in, all helping to revitalise the economy of the northern end of Raasay.'

It had taken a lifetime, but an official at council headquarters in Inverness had finally spelled out the words 'to revitalise the economy of the northern end of Raasay'.

In February 1982 the Scottish Development Department approved a grant of £101,612 to Highland Regional Council towards improving and surfacing the road between Brochel Castle and Arnish. The road squad began, as Calum MacLeod had himself begun two decades earlier, at Brochel. They were constrained by the fact that their heavy machinery could do yet further damage to the Arnish crofter's piece of land art, and by the fear that if they did venture out onto it, they might not get back again: 'there are no turning areas sufficient for vehicles to manoeuvre and turn round and it is doubtful whether the track in its present condition would stand up to the passage of contruction vehicles'.

The road was finished, more or less, by the end of 1982. Between Brochel Castle and a turning place a hundred yards above Calum and Lexie MacLeod's crofthouse in South Arnish there lay at the end of that year almost two miles of smooth and navigable road. It was a single-track highway, of course, but it had twenty passing places to permit the safe transit of northbound and southbound traffic. There were already plans to install sheep and cattle grids instead of gates to keep different townships' stock separate, all of which were located, purchased, installed and maintained by Calum MacLeod.

It was a road. 'People have lost much of the work that Calum had done,' said John Nicolson in unconscious echo of Magnus Magnusson and the artist Campbell Sandilands, 'because when the council started on the road to get it ready for tarring, they covered everything over.'

But it was a road. 'He was chuffed to bits,' said his daughter. 'He had a road to his house. My mum wasn't well, she had rheumatoid and osteo-arthritis and she was very crippled – at one point she was wheelchair bound – and the road got her in and out of Arnish and off to her hospital appointments. It made a tremendous difference in that way.

'It also helped with getting his peats home. The last peat bank he was cutting was at the side of the road almost as far as the deer fence. He used to cut peat there to stop the peat level rising above the road. He only had one problem. When the road reached the peat bank, peat began to go missing, and he suddenly realised that all of his peat was going to be away beyond Brochel if he didn't do something about it. So he went up there with a whole pile of plastic sacks and his lunch bag, filled the sacks with peat, and then some kind person drove them home.'

It was a road upon which people could drive without palpitations. 'I go in the summer when the family are here,' said Jessie Nicolson. 'Och, the road doesn't bother me now – it's tarmacked. It's lovely in the summertime with the family.'

'People from outwith this area,' said John Nicolson, 'and even people from within this area, look back on it now and say what an extraordinary achievement. But in fact it didn't seem that extraordinary to Calum. It was a job that needed doing, and because no-one else was going to do it, he did it.

'That would be about it. Nobody else would dare to do it except himself. Not even us, and we were only then in our thirties, would ever have dreamed of building that road – never mind a man that was sixty. When you look at it carefully it becomes even more remarkable. Here was somebody who left school at fourteen, and you could say he was more or less self-taught. You can only wonder, what if that man had gone to university? But what he did . . . it's brilliant!'

In October 1982 a journalist telephoned Calum

MacLeod to ask for his opinions of the tarmacking of the final stages of his road. 'I am very pleased indeed,' said Calum. 'They have done a very good job.' He chuckled. 'It'll be like an autobahn when they've finished. Mind you, they have not had to change an inch of the lines. I had an Australian science master over here this year and he said that, considering the terrain, the lines of the road were the finest example of scientific engineering he had seen!'

On 8 December 1982 Calum MacLeod wrote a letter from Arnish to Ian Boag, the divisional engineer with the council's road department in Skye. 'Naturally I am delighted', he said, 'with the magnificent improvement done to the Brochel/Arnish road and wish to express my sincerest gratitude and thanks to you and all your staff for work that cannot be expressed in words.

'It may interest you to know that recently, a visitor from Cape Town told me that it is a marvellous feat in roadmaking, and highly praised your staff engaged thereon, for their quality.'

The Last Man Out of Arnish

Calum MacLeod – man, road-builder and writer – could be described as quintessentially Gaelic, the flag-bearer of past generations, not folding to bureaucracy but building a road with heroic determination.

Campbell Sandilands, art student, 1984

Calum MacLeod never really stopped working on his road. Once it had been improved, surfaced and adopted from Brochel to the turning and parking place at his croft in South Arnish, he began extending it to his very back door: a job which he not only completed but also paid to have tarred. And there was always some kind of maintenance; always cattle-grids to clear and paint; drains and culverts to clean.

But he had, both before and after 1982, another life. His reading and especially his writing, which had always been important to Calum, took on an extra dimension in his later years. For as long as his letters and articles to the newspapers had always been in his second language,

English, he had never been able to achieve full expression. Only once the need had passed to propagandise for his cause in a tongue that Inverness councillors would understand could he relax back into Gaelic.*

He began to contribute regular articles to the Gaelic quarterly magazine *Gairm*. He began to write Gaelic histories of his people. And once again, sixty years after the Celtic Society of New York medal had been mailed to Arnish, he began to win literary prizes. In 1978 he entered an essay titled 'An Gaidheal Gaisgeil' ('The Heroic Gael') in an annual competition organised by the Gaelic Books Council in Glasgow. It won third prize.

* Coming as he did from a world in which everybody spoke Gaelic, most people spoke extremely fluent Gaelic and some people spoke only Gaelic, Calum MacLeod was exceptionally articulate in the language. In the 1980s Cailean Maclean conducted several Gaelic interviews with him for BBC radio. 'The last one', said Maclean, 'was a long interview about fishing in which he named what seemed like every boat between Shieldaig and Kyle on the mainland and Portree in Skye. He explained their different styles and how their shape altered, and the way they would behave at sea. He recalled counting twenty-eight boats tied together one night at shelter in the harbour at Rona. Remarkably, he also talked of impressive boats he had seen which were based in Scalpay and Castlebay in the Western Isles. He mentions one from the latter called the *St Columba*, and on his last trip to Barra – at least the last before the interview with me – he thought he saw her ribs rotting on the shore.

'The other remarkable thing about this interview was the fact that he spoke for about nine minutes, without hesitation, repetition or deviation, in answer to the first question. His Gaelic was also beautifully correct. Unusually in the late twentieth century, he very rarely used English words in his speech and mainly only to clarify if the Gaelic rendering that he had given might be ambiguous. For instance, he talked about a boat with a "lion cuairteachaidh", and then said in English: "a ring-net, as it is termed".'

He worked harder. He began to prepare a long essay which he would call 'Fasachadh Andiochdmhor Ratharsaigh', or 'The Cruel Clearances of Raasay'. 'My father didn't have any Highers,' said Julia Mac-Leod Allan, 'but my mother had her Higher Gaelic and Latin, so my mother used to help my father quite a bit. He was sometimes sticky with the Gaelic grammar. The main Gaelic book was the Bible, and once you could read the Bible end-to-end in Gaelic, you were fluent enough in Gaelic. But it all affected his style. I know that in "The Cruel Clearances of Raasay" some of the Gaelic is in Biblical style. He used to say to my mother, "How do you put this?" and "How do you put that, Lexie?" He used to write in the front room in Arnish. The table in that room was covered with references, books, letters to and from America, New Zealand, Australia . . . a huge network of correspondents, an enormous network, often of distant relatives abroad. So he had all that to keep up as well.'

In 1984 Calum explained how he had researched and written 'Fasachadh Andiochdmhor Ratharsaigh' in South Arnish. 'I had to contact Australian, New Zealand, Canadian and USA authorities,' he said. 'For instance, I had to get lists of emigrants on sailing ships. How these poor people fared, some drowned, others murdered, and others went insane on seeing the wildernesses to which they were sent, while those that went to Canada had to endure winters there clothed in rags and old sacks. I was shocked to learn the naked truth of which only a mere fraction has ever been published . . . Some dupes maintain that these Clearances did good to the Highlands, but that is downright ignorance of the horrors and cruelty involved [which were] typical of the revolting Spanish Inquisition, and hardly believable to have existed in a nation at least nominally Christian, or civilised.'

In 1982 – which was altogether an extremely satisfactory year for Calum MacLeod – 'Fasachadh Andiochdmhor Ratharsaigh' won joint first prize in the Gaelic Books Council's competition, and Calum received a cheque for £75.

The accolades were only beginning. In the New Year's Honours List of 1983 Calum was awarded the British Empire Medal. This merit was officially given to him as a reward for his decades of 'community service' both to the post office and to the Northern Lighthouse Board, decades which stretched from his time as a deckhand on the Rona lighthouse tender in the 1920s to his retirement in July 1975, when the Rona light was automated. Letters of congratulations – more than sixty of them – flooded into Arnish from the rest of Britain, from the USA, Canada and Australia. Calum MacLeod, wearing his full lighthouse dress uniform, was officially invested with the British Empire Medal by the lord lieutenant of Ross and Cromarty, Admiral Sir John Hayes, at a ceremony in southern Raasay in April 1983. Apologies for their unavoidable absence were received and noted from Queen Elizabeth II, from Mr Russell Johnston MP, and from the convener of the Highland Regional

Council, Mr Ian Campbell of Sligachan in Skye.

Mr Alastair Henry of the Department of Agriculture took the opportunity to comment on the 'extremely good order' of Calum MacLeod's croft. A cousin of Calum's from Brisbane in Australia travelled to be in attendance. In his presentation speech Admiral Hayes remarked that he had been a shipmate of Calum's late brother Ronald on board the aircraft carrier HMS *Indomitable* during the Second World War. Calum himself would muse that he was not the first member of his family to receive a medal. 'My cousin was the famous Captain Donald MacRae,' he said afterwards, 'the Sydney harbourmaster who was decorated twice before his death in 1962. He led an Australian contingent in the Dardanelles [during the First World War], and was said to be the last man out of Gallipoli, with a captured Turkish machine gun under his arm! His mother was born and brought up on what is now my very own holding in Arnish, and until his death Donald MacRae had more Gaelic than English.'

If Captain Donald MacRae's medal-winning feats had been clearly defined in the bloodbath of Gallipoli, his cousin Calum's was a masked award. Calum MacLeod's great achievement by 1983 was acknowledged to be the creation of his road, not his service to the Northern Lighthouse Board. But to have confirmed an emblem of twenty years' active agitprop against local and central government as sound reason to be offered the British Empire Medal might have set an embarrassing precedent. The citation said that he became Malcolm Mac-

Leod, BEM, for maintaining supplies to the Rona light, and latterly for working as local assistant keeper there for eight years. But the whole world knew that he had become Malcolm MacLeod, BEM, for building Calum's road. Following the presentation ceremony in the Isle of Raasay Hotel on the afternoon of Saturday, 23 April 1983 the entire official contingent drove north, and made its way in stately convoy along the finished road between Brochel and Arnish. 'They were very charmed with it,' said Calum MacLeod. 'But I never thought I'd end up with a British Empire Medal.' The establishment had, in a roundabout way, apologised.

And as the whole world could now make its way to Calum's door, the whole world did. 'The most I ever served in the house in Arnish', said Julia MacLeod Allan, 'was seventeen people. Mum and Dad, my husband and myself and our family, and ten others! We started off with chicken and potatoes, and I think peas and sweetcorn. Then – "Oh, dear, we're going to have to open a tin of ham . . . put some pineapple in as well" . . . and we kept taking out more plates and taking out more food, but we managed to feed seventeen people and it all started off with one chicken. It was one of these things Arnish was very good at!'

When, in 1984, the future artist and calligrapher Campbell Sandilands visited Arnish to prepare his dissertation for Duncan of Jordanstone College of Art he found his subject 'compiling a book on "The Great Men of Raasay", which consists of a series of short biographies on the "Sons of Raasay", who were all acquaintances of Calum during their lifetimes, and who plied their trades as policemen, soldiers, sailors, postmen and crofters.

'Calum MacLeod – man, road-builder and writer – could be described as quintessentially Gaelic, the flag-bearer of past generations, not folding to bureaucracy but building a road with heroic determination in spite of what the critics said, in spite of the bureaucrats . . . he is a man who writes passionately of his own people, seeing each individual in his own right. Because of his own extraordinary achievements he has won the distinction of becoming a hero in his own lifetime.'

The parable was almost complete. In 1986 the celebrated climber, naturalist, explorer, broadcaster and writer Tom Weir spent a day in South Arnish. 'The man I was eager to speak to', Weir would record, 'was the road-builder extraordinary, Calum MacLeod, but it took me three visits to his croft at Arnish before I found him at home, as he was so busy with his sheep.'

He remained, as Tom Weir discovered, fully active in his seventies. 'The coastguard used to phone', said Julia MacLeod Allan, 'with a report of a sheep on a cliff – "Could you check if this is real or is it just a hoax call?" – so he would be traipsing off down to the shores of Umachan or Kyle Rona to check these things. Or people would phone him to ask him to get in touch with somebody taking a holiday in one of the old houses on Fladda – as if Fladda was next door – because after the phone box was taken away we had the only telephone in the north end.'

'At 74 years of age,' wrote Tom Weir, 'and after 47 years in the lighthouse service, he is a good advertisement for Raasay. He is a natural scholar and historian, though his only schooling was at Torran which he left at 14. He married the school's last teacher whose pupils had reached the stage where they could be counted on one hand.

'Talking about depopulation of the roadless north end, he told me: "When I began on the road there were seven families at this end. When I finished it 10 years later there were only ourselves. I hope the road will bring people here to settle again. A retired couple have already done so, and I think it would be a good thing if Raasay people who have worked away from the island, and who want to come back to retire, were given a small holding and the right to build a house."

'He told me about his own life: at 16 working as a deck boy on the attendance boat serving Rona lighthouse, eventually becoming its master, and then becoming a lighthouse keeper on Rona, a rock station at which he did duty for a month on and a month off.*

' "It makes me proud when I see vehicles now where before you couldn't take a handbarrow. I counted 20 cars going past when I was working at the sheep yesterday, and I've seen 17 in the car park." '

Tom Weir and his wife spent six hours talking to Calum and Lexie MacLeod, and their daughter Julia, and Julia's children, in Arnish in the summer of 1986.

---

* Calum manned the Rona light for a month on and a fortnight off.

They were shown Calum's 'vast collection of photographs, some of people evicted from the island.

'He corresponds', wrote Weir, 'with around 28 families in Australia, New Zealand, Cape Town, the USA and Canada, descendants of people cleared from Raasay between 1851 and 1854. Since the road was built, many visitors from abroad, descended from evicted islanders, have called on him.'

A year and a half after Tom Weir's visit, on Tuesday, 26 January, 1988, Calum MacLeod finished his midday meal and went outside to continue working. 'He'd had his lunch,' said his daughter, 'and went out of the door, but he didn't come back in for his mid-afternoon cuppa.

'My mother thought he was busy doing something, or had met somebody and would be chatting. Then she realised that it was getting dark and wondered, "Where is he? The cows have to be fed." She took her Zimmer frame or her walking sticks and went outside, and all the cows were at the end of the house looking through the gate. She wondered what the cows were doing there, and she looked further round to find my father there, just at the end of our house. He was in his wheelbarrow, with Coll, the white collie, on watch.

'I think he had sat down on the wheelbarrow because he felt unwell. We assume it was a heart attack. The family was prone to them. It probably was a heart attack – cholesterol, all these things we hear about now.

'Father contemplated what would happen to him without my mother, but I don't think my mother ever in her wildest thoughts imagined that he would go first.

My father was that well and my mother was not. He would find her lying on the floor, and that used to frighten my father. She wasn't allowed to go upstairs if he was outside.

'But at the end of the day, she was the one who had to go out and find him. It was miraculous that he was only at the end of the house and not out on one of his walks on the hills.'

Due to the death of a bull, nobody would ever know exactly what had killed Calum MacLeod. Nine months before his death, in April 1987, three men from the small island of Vatersay in the Outer Hebrides transported an Aberdeen Angus bull belonging to the Department of Agriculture to their grazings to inseminate their forty cattle. The men took the bull to Vatersay in what was then both the traditional and the only feasible manner. They towed it, swimming, from a rope attached to the stern of a rowing boat across the 300 yards of sea between Vatersay and its larger neighbouring island of Barra.

The bull drowned. The three men were subsequently charged under the Protection of Animals (Scotland) Act. They appeared at Lochmaddy Sheriff Court in North Uist to answer those charges on Wednesday, 27 January 1988. The area's procurator fiscal was obliged to be in North Uist on that day, the day after the death of Calum MacLeod of South Arnish in Raasay, in order to prosecute the charges. He did so unsuccessfully: the three Vatersay men were found Not Guilty.

There is no separate coroner or system of coroners'

courts in Scotland. It is the function of the Procurator Fiscal Service not only to prosecute criminal offences but also to investigate sudden deaths. In the definition of the Scottish Crown Office, 'It is the duty of the appropriate Procurator Fiscal to enquire into all sudden, suspicious, accidental, unexpected and unexplained deaths and in particular into all deaths resulting from an accident in the course of employment or occupation.' On other occasions, the procurator fiscal might have signed an order for a post mortem into the death of Calum MacLeod. He did not do so partly because he was that week in North Uist unsuccessfully pressing the case of the Department of Agriculture's Aberdeen Angus stud.

'As to whether my father died from a coronary thrombosis or a stroke or an aneurism or what', said his daughter, 'we will never know . . . in one way it might be useful to know. But he was dead, so it was hypothetical.'

Calum MacLeod was laid to rest on Friday, 29 January 1988 in a graveyard in the south end of Raasay on a wooded hillside facing east. He was seventy-six years old. He was joined by his wife, Lexie, who had lived to within three months of her ninetieth birthday, in January 2001.

Unlike previous generations and unlike his own father, Calum MacLeod did not have to be taken by boat from Arnish to the cemetery in southern Raasay. The hearse was driven to his door.

'Calum was the last man to come out of Arnish',

said his former neighbour Donald MacLeod, 'down the road he built with his own hands.'

* * *

A dry-stone cairn stands on the hilltop above Brochel Castle, a fifth of a mile up the adopted council road to Arnish. It is built of large blocks of Raasay granite. A plaque is affixed to the side of the cairn which faces the passing highway. The inscription upon it reads, in two languages:

RATHAD CHALUIM

RE IOMADH BLIADHNA B'E SEO AM FRITH-RATHAD GU ARNAIS
$1^3/_4$ MILE CHAIDH A LEUDACHADH AGUS A' DHEASACHADH
GU RATHAD
MOR LE IONADAN LEIG SEACHAD GU IRE TEARRAIDH LE
CALUM MACLEOID. B.E.M.
(1911–1988)
ARNAIS MU DHEAS
SHAOTHRAICH E NA AONAR AGUS CHUIR ECRIOCH
AIR AN OBAIR AN CHEANN DEICH BLIADHNA

CALUM'S ROAD

THIS FORMER FOOTPATH TO ARNISH – A DISTANCE OF $1^3/_4$
MILES – WAS WIDENED TO A SINGLE TRACK ROAD WITH
PASSING PLACES AND PREPARED FOR SURFACING BY
MALCOLM MACLEOD. B.E.M.
(1911–1988)
SOUTH ARNISH
HE ACCOMPLISHED THIS WORK SINGLE-HANDEDLY
OVER A PERIOD OF TEN YEARS

To the south of the cairn the reckless panorama of eastern Raasay unfolds. Cliffsides and waterfalls tumble down to the sea from high pastures above the empty ruins of Screapadal and Hallaig. To the north of the cairn the black road which leads to Arnish switchbacks smoothly over the moor. From that vantage point, it appears to be the beginning of a long journey.

Notes

Chapter One

The Island of Strong Men

pp. 5–6: 'There is bad weather . . . don't have them here.' Interview with Alan Hamilton for BBC radio programme 'Our Wild Peregrination', broadcast 7 October 1980

pp. 6–7: 'this little isle . . . in Circumference' Martin Martin, *A Description of the Western Islands of Scotland*, p. 165

p. 7: 'Raasay is . . . solitary herdsman.' Samuel Johnson, *A Journey to the Western Islands of Scotland*, p. 53

p. 7: 'The north . . . a pavement.' James Boswell, *Journal of a Tour to the Hebrides*, p. 122

p. 9: 'the green . . . western coast.' John MacCulloch, *Description of the Western Islands of Scotland, including the Isle of Man*, p. 132

p. 13: 'The coast . . . in clambering.' *The Scotsman*, 23 May 1883

pp. 15–30: Evidence to Napier Commission given in Torran Schoolhouse, 22 May 1883, extracted from Minutes of Evidence to Highlands and Islands Commission, pp. 438–474

pp. 33–34: 'At one time . . . in 1929.' Charles MacLeod in interview with author, 2005

p. 34: 'Donald's wife . . . being careful.' John Nicolson, *I Remember*, p. 62

p. 35: 'He must . . . school day.' *ibid.*, p. 93

pp. 35–36: 'Mr MacKinnon ran . . . the place.' John Cumming, interviewed by Timothy Neat in *When I Was Young: The Islands*, p. 24

p. 36: 'children at . . . English language.' *I Remember*, p. 94

pp. 37–38: 'That was how . . . we called it.' John Nicolson in interview with author, 2005

p. 38: 'When I was . . . if not more.' BBC radio programme 'Our Wild Peregrination'

p. 38–39: 'One evening . . . me in bed!' BBC radio programme 'Our Wild Peregrination'

p. 40: 'In my younger . . . the saying goes.' Interview with Derek Cooper for BBC television programme 'The Island That Nearly Made It', broadcast 5 June 1973

Chapter Two

The Book of Hours

p. 45: 'we will take . . . little children' 'Revealed after 60 years – the story of the Raasay land raids', *West Highland Free Press*, 8 January 1982

p. 46: 'took possession . . . for the lands.' *The Scotsman*, 7 October 1921

p. 47: 'erected several . . . of the island.' *The Scotsman*, 3 August 1921

p. 47–48: 'The men repudiate . . . longer in Rona.' *The Scotsman*, 3 August 1931

p. 48–49: 'some pathetic . . . prison gates' *The Scotsman*, 21 September 1921

p. 49: 'Although the hour . . . about 40' *The Scotsman*, 23 September 1921

p. 49: 'in some respects . . . difficult' *The Scotsman*, 7 October 1921

p. 50: 'It is impossible . . . of Heaven.' 'Revealed after 60 years . . .' *West Highland Free Press*

p. 51: 'a large crowd . . . mainland.' *The Scotsman*, 23 December 1921

p. 55: 'a rather gloomy . . . Rona' John Cumming, 'Reminiscences!', *Skyeviews* (Issue 8), 1996 pp. 55–56: 'Peggy Benton . . . the island.' *ibid.*

p. 58: 'I found . . . carrying guns.' *ibid.*

pp. 58–61: 'The thing that . . . or wherever.' John Nicolson in interview with author, 2005

pp. 61–62: 'It was a . . . crowd did.' *ibid.*

p. 62: 'we were . . . being late.' John Cumming, interviewed in *When I Was Young: The Islands*, p. 24

p. 63: 'Wood would . . . the herring.' John Nicolson in interview with author, 2005

p. 64: 'They used . . . it happened.' *ibid.*

p. 66: 'They got . . . coming in.' *ibid.*

p. 67: 'The townships . . . fortunate crofter.' *I Remember*, p. 31

pp. 68–69: 'by residenters . . . or thereby' Minutes of Roads Committee of Inverness County Council, 23 September 1931

p. 73: 're-submitted . . . own tenants.' *ibid.*

p. 75–76: 'should consider . . . matter meantime' Minutes of Roads Committee of Inverness County Council, 16 November 1934

pp. 76–77: 'It was . . . cart road.' *I Remember*, p. 63

p. 77: 'The people . . . to Inverarish.' 'Reminiscences!'

p. 78: 'When they left . . . after the war.' John Nicolson in interview with author, 2005

Chapter Three

A Few in the North Would Not Be Catered For

p. 79: 'Now, if . . . a wee turn.' John Nicolson in interview with author, 2005

p. 81: 'was a very . . . was declared' Letter from Lexie MacLeod to her grandson, undated

p. 81: 'By 1941 . . . my age.' John Nicolson in interview with author, 2005

pp. 83–84: 'All of the . . . Skye name.' Julia MacLeod Allan in interview with author, 2005

p. 84: 'The one and . . . cooking.' *I Remember*, p. 117

pp. 84–85: 'She was . . . appointment.' Julia MacLeod Allan in interview with author, 2005

pp. 85–86: 'No broad . . . a few days.' Letter from Lexie MacLeod to her grandson

pp. 86–87: 'He was once . . . the hands went.' John Nicolson in interview with author, 2005

p. 88–89: ''N am cogadh . . . usual tobacco.' Calum MacLeod in interview with Cailean Maclean for BBC Radio Scotland, 1986

p. 90: 'some time ago . . . catered for.' Letter from NOSHEB to Inverness County Council, 29 October 1954

pp. 90–91: 'well the . . . six o'clock news.' Julia MacLeod Allan in interview with author, 2005

pp. 92–93: 'with our . . . final make-up.' *ibid.*

pp. 93–94: 'Fladda was . . . very passable.' Charles MacLeod in interview with author, 2005

p. 95: 'Everybody's all . . . Calum did.' John Nicolson in interview with author, 2005

p. 96: 'intimated . . . Public Highway.' Minutes of Roads Committee of Inverness County Council, 10 October 1950

pp. 96–97: 'The Engineer . . . relation to use.' Letter from Lt Col Neil McLean, Scottish Office, Whitehall, 5 June 1962

pp. 97–98: 'After the Second . . . no other work.' John Nicolson in interview with author, 2005

pp. 98–99: 'We started . . . with breaks.' Julia MacLeod Allan in interview with author, 2005

pp. 99–100: 'It wasn't really . . . you might say.' Jessie Nicolson in interview with author, 2005

pp. 100–101: 'Calum took . . . think back on.' *ibid.*

p. 101: 'As far as . . . in jail!' John Nicolson in interview with author, 2005

pp. 101–102: 'We got all . . . lots of things.' Jessie Nicolson in interview with author, 2005

pp. 102–104: 'There were three . . . Closed Brethren.' Julia MacLeod Allan in interview with author, 2005

p. 105: 'When we came . . . education . . . no!' John Nicolson in interview with author, 2005

pp. 105–106: 'got a letter . . . my primary.' Julia MacLeod Allan in interview with author, 2005

p. 107: 'You were taken . . . my abilities!' *ibid.*

pp. 107–109: 'Another factor . . . of their homes.' Calum MacLeod, 'The Ruination of Raasay', *West Highland Free Press*, 14 September 1973

Chapter Four

No Chance of Being Run Down by a Car

pp. 111–112: 'In the 50s . . . trying to do.' John Nicolson in interview with author, 2005

p. 115: 'After the war . . . County Council.' *ibid.*

pp. 115–116: 'The Royal Engineers . . . ever used.' *West Highland Free Press*, 16 February 1979

p. 119: 'by hand to . . . road surface.' Campbell Sandilands, 'Calum's Road'

p. 121: 'With the . . . Arnish as well.' *Oban Times*, 25 December 1964

p. 122: 'Oh, it was . . . much so.' Jessie Nicolson in interview with author, 2005

p. 122–123: 'My father . . . straight home.' Julia MacLeod Allan in interview with author, 2005

p. 124: 'Is it any . . . and Islands.' *Stornoway Gazette*, 22 April 1967

pp. 124–126: 'Socialism . . . and Islands.' Calum MacLeod, letter to *Stornoway Gazette*, 9 May 1970

p. 127: 'We were . . . the community.' Jessie Nicolson in interview with author, 2005

p. 128: 'He was . . . up on it.' *ibid.*

p. 128: 'I don't think . . . for progress.' Julia MacLeod Allan in interview with author, 2005

p. 128: 'Lexie wasn't . . . he finished.' John Nicolson in interview with author, 2005

p. 130: 'When you saw . . . to do.' *ibid.*

pp. 130–131: 'There were two . . . that pinnacle.' Julia MacLeod Allan in interview with author, 2005

p. 131: 'Oh, there was . . . it all in.' Jessie Nicolson in interview with author, 2005

p. 132: 'I started . . . measure rainfall.' *West Highland Free Press*, 22 January 1982

p. 134: 'with tulips . . . the cliffs.' D. A. Maclean in Derek Cooper, *Skye*, p. 33

p. 138: 'It was . . . his grandchildren!' Julia MacLeod Allan in interview with author, 2005

pp. 138–139: 'Of course . . . burn out.' *ibid.*

pp. 139–140: 'Before me . . . Homosexual Bills?' Calum Mac-Leod, *Stornoway Gazette*, 26 October 1970

p. 141: 'Oh, plantlife! . . . in Kent.' Calum MacLeod in interview with Derek Cooper for BBC TV programme 'The Island That Nearly Made It', broadcast 5 June 1973

p. 142: 'The voice of . . . prize-winning essay.' *Daily Telegraph*, 28 May 1972

pp. 143–147: 'A few months . . . but to himself.' BBC TV programme 'The Island That Nearly Made It'

p. 148: 'I was digging . . . in Denmark.' Calum MacLeod in interview with Ian Grimble for BBC TV programme 'Grimble on Islands: Raasay', broadcast 2 October 1984

pp. 150–151: 'Not far . . . he did that.' Donald MacLeod, interviewed in *When I Was Young: The Islands*', p. 1

Chapter Five

A Kind of Historical Justification

p. 153: 'My husband . . . best of times.' Jessie Nicolson in interview with author, 2005

p. 154: 'I remember . . . achievement!' John Nicolson in interview with author, 2005

p. 154: 'Calum's road . . . original form.' Magnus Magnusson, 'The Road That Calum Built', *Today*, March/April 1982

p. 154: 'It will . . . lovely area.' Campbell Sandilands, 'Calum's Road'

pp. 154–155: 'I don't . . . Calum now.' 'The Road That Calum Built'

p. 156: 'I would not . . . the EEC.' Alistair Nicolson, *West Highland Free Press*, 9 November 1973

pp. 160–161: 'is officially . . . about it.' 'The Road That Calum Built'

pp. 161–162: 'When Calum's . . . the cost.' Sam MacNaughton, email to author, 27 January 2006

p. 170: 'People have . . . everything over.' John Nicolson in interview with author, 2005

pp. 170–171: 'He was chuffed . . . them home.' Julia MacLeod Allan in interview with author, 2005

p. 171: 'I go in . . . the family.' Jessie Nicolson in interview with author, 2005

p. 171: 'People from . . . it's brilliant!' *ibid.*

p. 172: 'I am very . . . he had seen.' Calum MacLeod interviewed in *West Highland Free Press*, 22 October 1982

Chapter Six

The Last Man Out of Arnish

p. 175: 'My father . . . as well.' Julia MacLeod Allan in interview with author, 2005

p. 175–176: 'I had to . . . or civilised.' Campbell Sandilands, 'Calum's Road'

p. 177: 'My cousin . . . than English.' Calum MacLeod in *West Highland Free Press*, 29 April 1983

p. 178: 'The most . . . good at!' Julia MacLeod Allan in interview with author, 2005

p. 179: 'Calum MacLeod . . . own lifetime.' Campbell Sandilands, 'Calum's Road'

p. 179: 'The man . . . his sheep.' Tom Weir, 'Return to Raasay', *Scots Magazine*, October 1986

p. 179: 'The coastguard . . . north end.' *ibid.*

p. 180: 'At 74 years . . . the car park.' *ibid.*

p. 181: 'He corresponds . . . on him.' *ibid.*

pp. 181–182: 'He'd had . . . on the hills.' Julia MacLeod Allan in interview with author, 2005

p. 183: 'As to whether . . . hypothetical.' *ibid.*

pp. 183–184: 'Calum was . . . own hands.' Donald MacLeod, interviewed in *When I Was Young: The Islands*, p. 1

Bibliography

Books, reports and unpublished material

Aitken, Thomas, *Road Making and Maintenance* (London, 1900)
Boswell, James, *Journal of a Tour to the Hebrides* (London, 1785)
Cameron, A.D., *Go Listen to the Crofters* (Stornoway, 1986)
Cooper, Derek, *Hebridean Connection* (London, 1977) *Skye* (London, 1970)
Draper, Lawrence and Pamela, *The Raasay Iron Mine* (Dingwall, 1990)
HM Government, *Report of the Royal [Napier] Commission into Crofting* (London, 1884)
Hunter, James, *Last of the Free* (Edinburgh, 1999)
Johnson, Samuel, *A Journey to the Western Islands of Scotland* (London, 1775)
MacLeod, Norma, *Raasay* (Edinburgh, 2002)
MacCulloch, John, *A Description of the Western Islands of Scotland, Including the Isle of Man* (London, 1819)
Martin, Martin, *A Description of the Western Islands of Scotland* (London, 1703)
Neat, Timothy, *When I Was Young: The Islands* (Edinburgh, 2000)
Nicolson, John, *I Remember* (Edinburgh, 1989)
Raasay Heritage Society, *Duanagan, Dain is Dualchas a Eilean Ratharsair, Fladaidh is Eilean Tighe* (Raasay, 2001)

Sandilands, Campbell, 'Calum's Road', thesis for Duncan of Jordanstone College of Art, 1984

Sharpe, Richard, *Raasay* (London, 1978)

Newspapers and magazines

Daily Telegraph
Oban Times
Press and Journal
Scots Magazine
The Scotsman
Scottish Islands Explorer
Skyeviews
Stornoway Gazette
Today
West Highland Free Press

BIRLINN LTD (incorporating John Donald and Polygon) is one of Scotland's leading publishers with over four hundred titles in print. Should you wish to be put on our catalogue mailing list **contact**:

Catalogue Request
Birlinn Ltd
West Newington House
10 Newington Road
Edinburgh EH9 1QS
Scotland, UK

Tel: + 44 (0) 131 668 4371
Fax: + 44 (0) 131 668 4466
e-mail: info@birlinn.co.uk

Postage and packing is free within the UK. For overseas orders, postage and packing (airmail) will be charged at 30% of the total order value.

For more information, or to order online, visit our website at **www.birlinn.co.uk**

IMPRINTS: JOHN DONALD · POLYGON